Francis Frith's
GREATER MANCHESTER

PHOTOGRAPHIC MEMORIES

Francis Frith's
GREATER MANCHESTER

◆

Clive Hardy

FRITH
BOOK CO

First published in the United Kingdom in 2000 by
Frith Book Company Ltd

Hardback Edition 2000
ISBN 1-85937-108-6

Paperback Edition 2000
ISBN 1-85937-266-x

Reprinted in paperback 2002

Reprinted in hardback 2003

British Library Cataloguing in Publication Data

Francis Frith's Greater Manchester
Clive Hardy

Frith Book Company Ltd
Frith's Barn, Teffont,
Salisbury, Wiltshire SP3 5QP
Tel: +44 (0) 1722 716 376
Email: info@francisfrith.co.uk
www.francisfrith.co.uk

Printed and bound in Great Britain

AS WITH ANY HISTORICAL DATABASE THE FRITH ARCHIVE IS CONSTANTLY BEING CORRECTED AND IMPROVED
AND THE PUBLISHERS WOULD WELCOME INFORMATION ON OMISSIONS OR INACCURACIES

CONTENTS

◆

FRANCIS FRITH: *Victorian Pioneer*

FRANCIS FRITH, Victorian founder of the world-famous photographic archive, was a complex and multitudinous man. A devout Quaker and a highly successful Victorian businessman, he was both philosophic by nature and pioneering in outlook.

By 1855 Francis Frith had already established a wholesale grocery business in Liverpool, and sold it for the astonishing sum of £200,000, which is the equivalent today of over £15,000,000. Now a multi-millionaire, he was able to indulge his passion for travel. As a child he had pored over travel books written by early explorers, and his fancy and imagination had been stirred by family holidays to the sublime mountain regions of Wales and Scotland. 'What a land of spirit-stirring and enriching scenes and places!' he had written. He was to return to these scenes of grandeur in later years to 'recapture the thousands of vivid and tender memories', but with a different purpose. Now in his thirties, and captivated by the new science of photography, Frith set out on a series of pioneering journeys to the Nile regions that occupied him from 1856 until 1860.

INTRIGUE AND ADVENTURE

He took with him on his travels a specially-designed wicker carriage that acted as both dark-room and sleeping chamber. These far-flung journeys were packed with intrigue and adventure. In his life story, written when he was sixty-three, Frith tells of being held captive by bandits, and of fighting 'an awful midnight battle to the very point of surrender with a deadly pack of hungry, wild dogs'. Sporting flowing Arab costume, Frith arrived at Akaba by camel seventy years before Lawrence, where he encountered 'desert princes and rival sheikhs, blazing with jewel-hilted swords'.

During these extraordinary adventures he was assiduously exploring the desert regions bordering the Nile and patiently recording the antiquities and peoples with his camera. He was the first photographer to venture beyond the sixth cataract. Africa was still the mysterious 'Dark Continent', and Stanley and Livingstone's historic meeting was a decade into the future. The conditions for picture taking confound belief. He laboured for hours in his wicker dark-room in the sweltering heat of the desert, while the volatile chemicals fizzed dangerously in their trays. Often he was forced to work in remote tombs and caves where conditions were cooler. Back in London he exhibited his photographs and was 'rapturously cheered' by members of the Royal Society. His reputation as a photographer was made overnight. An eminent modern historian has likened their impact on the population of the time to that on our own generation of the first photographs taken on the surface of the moon.

VENTURE OF A LIFE-TIME

Characteristically, Frith quickly spotted the opportunity to create a new business as a specialist publisher of photographs. He lived in an era of immense and sometimes violent change. For the poor in the early part of Victoria's reign work was a drudge and the hours long, and people had precious little free time to enjoy themselves.

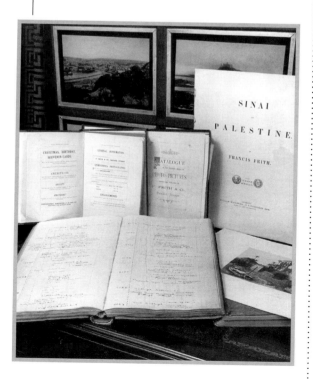

Most had no transport other than a cart or gig at their disposal, and had not travelled far beyond the boundaries of their own town or village. However, by the 1870s, the railways had threaded their way across the country, and Bank Holidays and half-day Saturdays had been made obligatory by Act of Parliament. All of a sudden the ordinary working man and his family were able to enjoy days out and see a little more of the world.

With characteristic business acumen, Francis Frith foresaw that these new tourists would enjoy having souvenirs to commemorate their days out. In 1860 he married Mary Ann Rosling and set out with the intention of photographing every city, town and village in Britain. For the next thirty years he travelled the country by train and by pony and trap, producing fine photographs of seaside resorts and beauty spots that were keenly bought by millions of Victorians. These prints were painstakingly pasted into family albums and pored over during the dark nights of winter, rekindling precious memories of summer excursions.

THE RISE OF FRITH & CO

Frith's studio was soon supplying retail shops all over the country. To meet the demand he gathered about him a small team of photographers, and published the work of independent artist-photographers of the calibre of Roger Fenton and Francis Bedford. In order to gain some understanding of the scale of Frith's business one only has to look at the catalogue issued by Frith & Co in 1886: it runs to some 670

pages, listing not only many thousands of views of the British Isles but also many photographs of most European countries, and China, Japan, the USA and Canada – note the sample page shown above from the hand-written *Frith & Co* ledgers detailing pictures taken. By 1890 Frith had created the greatest specialist photographic publishing company in the world, with over 2,000 outlets – more than the combined number that Boots and WH Smith have today! The picture on the right shows the *Frith & Co* display board at Ingleton in the Yorkshire Dales. Beautifully constructed with mahogany frame and gilt inserts, it could display up to a dozen local scenes.

POSTCARD BONANZA

The ever-popular holiday postcard we know today took many years to develop. In 1870 the Post Office issued the first plain cards, with a pre-printed stamp on one face. In 1894 they allowed other publishers' cards to be sent through the mail with an attached adhesive halfpenny stamp. Demand grew rapidly, and in 1895 a new size of postcard was permitted called the court card, but there was little room for illustration. In 1899, a year after Frith's death, a new card measuring 5.5 x 3.5 inches became the standard format, but it was not until 1902 that the divided back came into being, with address and message on one face and a full-size illustration on the other. *Frith & Co* were in the vanguard of postcard development, and Frith's sons Eustace and Cyril continued their father's monumental task, expanding the number of views offered to the public and recording more and more places in Britain, as the coasts and countryside were opened up to mass travel.

Francis Frith died in 1898 at his villa in Cannes, his great project still growing. The archive he created continued in business for another seventy years. By 1970 it contained over a third of a million pictures of 7,000 cities, towns and villages. The massive photographic record Frith has left to us stands as a living monument to a special and very remarkable man.

Frith's Archive: *A Unique Legacy*

FRANCIS FRITH'S legacy to us today is of immense significance and value, for the magnificent archive of evocative photographs he created provides a unique record of change in 7,000 cities, towns and villages throughout Britain over a century and more. Frith and his fellow studio photographers revisited locations many times down the years to update their views, compiling for us an enthralling and colourful pageant of British life and character.

We tend to think of Frith's sepia views of Britain as nostalgic, for most of us use them to conjure up memories of places in our own lives with which we have family associations. It often makes us forget that to Francis Frith they were records of daily life as it was actually being lived in the cities, towns and villages of his day. The Victorian age was one of great and often bewildering change for ordinary people, and though the pictures evoke an impression of slower times, life was as busy and hectic as it is today.

We are fortunate that Frith was a photographer of the people, dedicated to recording the minutiae of everyday life. For it is this sheer wealth of visual data, the painstaking chronicle of changes in dress, transport, street layouts, buildings, housing, engineering and landscape that captivates us so much today. His remarkable images offer us a powerful link with the past and with the lives of our ancestors.

TODAY'S TECHNOLOGY

Computers have now made it possible for Frith's many thousands of images to be accessed almost instantly. In the Frith archive today, each photograph is carefully 'digitised' then stored on a CD Rom. Frith archivists can locate a single photograph amongst thousands within seconds. Views can be catalogued and sorted under a variety of categories of place and content to the immediate benefit of researchers. Inexpensive reference prints can be created for them at the touch of a mouse button, and a wide range of books and other printed materials assembled and published for a wider, more general readership - in the next twelve months over a hundred Frith local history titles will be published! The

See Frith at www.francisfrith.co.uk

day-to-day workings of the archive are very different from how they were in Francis Frith's time: imagine the herculean task of sorting through eleven tons of glass negatives as Frith had to do to locate a particular sequence of pictures! Yet the archive still prides itself on maintaining the same high standards of excellence laid down by Francis Frith, including the painstaking cataloguing and indexing of every view.

It is curious to reflect on how the internet now allows researchers in America and elsewhere greater instant access to the archive than Frith himself ever enjoyed. Many thousands of individual views can be called up on screen within seconds on one of the Frith internet sites, enabling people living continents away to revisit the streets of their ancestral home town, or view places in Britain where they have enjoyed holidays. Many overseas researchers welcome the chance to view special theme selections, such as transport, sports, costume and ancient monuments.

We are certain that Francis Frith would have heartily approved of these modern developments, for he himself was always working at the very limits of Victorian photographic technology.

THE VALUE OF THE ARCHIVE TODAY

Because of the benefits brought by the computer, Frith's images are increasingly studied by social historians, by researchers into genealogy and ancestry, by architects, town planners, and by teachers and schoolchildren involved in local history projects. In addition, the archive offers every one of

us a unique opportunity to examine the places where we and our families have lived and worked down the years. Immensely successful in Frith's own era, the archive is now, a century and more on, entering a new phase of popularity.

THE PAST IN TUNE WITH THE FUTURE

Historians consider the Francis Frith Collection to be of prime national importance. It is the only archive of its kind remaining in private ownership and has been valued at a million pounds. However, this figure is now rapidly increasing as digital technology enables more and more people around the world to enjoy its benefits.

Francis Frith's archive is now housed in an historic timber barn in the beautiful village of Teffont in Wiltshire. Its founder would not recognize the archive office as it is today. In place of the many thousands of dusty boxes containing glass plate negatives and an all-pervading odour of photographic chemicals, there are now ranks of computer screens. He would be amazed to watch his images travelling round the world at unimaginable speeds through network and internet lines.

The archive's future is both bright and exciting. Francis Frith, with his unshakeable belief in making photographs available to the greatest number of people, would undoubtedly approve of what is being done today with his lifetime's work. His photographs, depicting our shared past, are now bringing pleasure and enlightenment to millions around the world a century and more after his death.

GREATER MANCHESTER – *An Introduction*

FOR A THOUSAND years our county system had served England well, but in 1974 the Local Government Act 1972 came into effect; with it came a radical realignment of many of our county boundaries, with scant regard for history, tradition, community or identity. Yorkshire, our largest county, was dissected. The provisions of the Act saw the abolition of the three ridings, an administrative division that had served the county well since the days when it was ruled by its own Scandinavian kings at York. The ridings were replaced by three new counties, North Yorkshire, South Yorkshire and West Yorkshire. In addition, former East and West Riding territory was hived off to create something called Humberside; Lancashire and the new county of Cumbria gained parts of the western areas of the West Riding; and a part of the North Riding which included the great steel town of Middlesbrough was incorporated into the new county of Cleveland. Staffordshire, Worcestershire and Warwickshire would also be robbed of territory, as the Black Country, Birmingham, and Coventry were transferred into a new county to be known as the West Midlands. Warwickshire came off worst. At a

stroke the county lost not only a large area of territory, but its manufacturing and commercial heartland centred on Birmingham and Coventry. Cumberland and Westmorland were abolished altogether, and Rutland, England's smallest county, was dragged kicking and screaming into a merger with Leicestershire.

Southern Lancashire was butchered to create the Greater Manchester Metropolitan County and the Merseyside Metropolitan County. Greater Manchester absorbed the county boroughs of Wigan, Bolton, Bury, Rochdale, Oldham, Salford, and Manchester together with a host of non-county boroughs and urban and rural districts; it also absorbed a sizeable slice of Cheshire that included Stockport, Altrincham, Cheadle, Bowdon, and Bramhall. In return, Cheshire received Warrington and Widnes. Lancashire Life ran a competition to see which reader could come up with the most appropriate word to describe what was happening to their county. The winner was 'Lancastration'.

This book is divided into three sections. The first takes us round Barton-upon-Irwell, Eccles, Worsley, Wigan, Bolton, Bury,

Rochdale, and Delph. The earliest pictures, dating from 1889, were taken at Worsley. They include images of the Old Hall, where James Brindley lodged whilst working on the Bridgewater Canal; the Court House, which despite its looks is in fact a Victorian building; and the old Packet House, where passengers could take boat to Liverpool, Manchester, Wigan and Warrington. In the 1890s Frith cameramen travelled widely around Lancashire, and amongst the places they photographed were Bolton, Bury, Rochdale and Wigan.

The Bolton trip also included a visit to the then ivy-clad Smithill's Hall. Tradition says that the hall was built on the site of a chapel dedicated to the Blessed Virgin, consecrated in AD793 by the Bishop of Hexham, and that it was a house of the Knights Hospitaller of St John of Jerusalem in the late 12th century. At this date there were several divisions within the Order. The hospitaller role, the care of the sick and the welfare of pilgrims bound for the Holy Land, was fulfilled by brother priests and sisters. The fighting was done by the brother knights and sergeants. The hall was later home to the Radcliffes, the Bartons, and latterly the Byron family. It was Andrew Barton who extended the hall around 1516 and added the chapel. Another of the Bolton pictures is of the Town Hall, designed by William Hill, with its six-column portico of Corinthian columns and a tower topped off with a French cap. It is considered to be one of the finest classical-style civic buildings in Lancashire; the view was enhanced a few years ago when the exterior was cleaned for the first time.

By the mid 19th century Preston, Bolton, Blackburn, Burnley, Rochdale and Oldham were major players in the manufacture of cotton. Bolton was where Samuel Crompton had developed his spinning mule in 1779. This machine revolutionised the industry; there was less thread-breakage than with the spinning jenny, and it was also capable of producing the very finest yarn. The town was also where Richard Arkwright had worked as a

barber before going on to other things. Though the first power mill in Bolton opened in the 1780s, Rochdale, a member of the coarse-spinning group of towns, was slow to adopt power weaving. It also continued to maintain a considerable woollen industry. In the 16th century the woollen towns of Rochdale, Burnley, Bolton, and Colne had a largest concentration of coarse-spinning mills in the county, but its success depended large-ly on exports. After the Great War both the cotton and woollen industries would go into a decline. Between 1929 and 1966, mill employ-ment in Oldham would drop by 70 per cent. Bolton fared better: its fine-spinning mills weathered Asian competition and decline was

combined output of several thousand yards of cloth a week, much of which went to the Rossendale Valley for finishing. The woollen industry was so vital to the country's economy that an Act of Parliament was passed in 1667 to stimulate home trade. One of its more unusual features is that it became illegal to bury a corpse in 'shirt, sheet, shroud or shift, but in woollen' on pain of a fine of £5, a con-siderable amount of money. The Act was still in force in 1709 when Thomas Warburton of Hale chose to bury his wife in a linen shroud. A wealthy man, Thomas handed over £5 'to ye churchwardens of Bowdon for ye use of ye poor'.

Of all the spinning towns, it was Oldham that grew the fastest. By the 1920s it had the

at a much slower rate. One of the pictures in this book is of Rochdale in 1913. In it are numerous mill chimneys; how many are left today? There are also several pictures of Healey Dell and Hollingworth Lake, both popular places where workers could get a breath of fresh air. Healey Dell, with its Fairy Chapel, was where Byron took Miss Mary Ann Chaworth, a kinswoman of his with whom he was in love. Byron was trying to win her heart, but he had a problem. William Byron, Fifth Lord of Newstead Abbey, had killed William Chaworth in a duel at the Star and Garter Hotel, London, in January 1765. (William was more than a little eccentric. He took great delight in hand-feeding crickets, but if they upset him he would punish them by spanking them with a blade of straw). As family memories in those days were a lot longer than they are today, Byron believed that wooing Miss Chaworth might prove an uphill task.

The final pictures in this section were taken around Delph in the mid 1950s. Delph lies within Saddleworth, which covers an area of 35 square miles. In the 19th century, though Delph lay within the parish of Rochdale, it was situated in the south-west extremity of the West Riding of Yorkshire. Within its four quarters, or meres, were 70 hamlets and villages, the largest being Delph and Dobcross. Delph was described as 'a good sized village with Methodist and Independent chapels, one mile north-west of Dobcross; there is a receiving house for letters'. Dobcross was slightly larger; it boasted two banks, a chapel, and a stamp and post office.

The second part of the book concentrates on Manchester itself. Frith cameramen visited the city in c1876, 1885, 1886, 1887, 1889, 1892, 1894 and 1895. The earliest pictures are of the Victoria Building (new in 1876) and of Owen's College, which had moved from Quay Street to its new purpose-built site on Oxford Road in 1873. The college had first opened its doors in 1851 thanks to merchant John Owen, who had left nearly £100,000 for the founding of the institution. The 1885 and 1886 pictures cover Market Street, St Ann's Square, the Royal Exchange, the Assize Court, and Piccadilly. Several pictures were taken of the infirmary in Piccadilly, but alas none were taken of the often appalling housing conditions in which many Mancunians were forced to live. Manchester was unhealthy well into the second half of the 19th century, though in 1868 it and Liverpool were the only places in Lancashire to have medical officers of health.

It took the Public Health Acts of 1872 and 1875 to galvanise the rest of the county into action and establish urban and rural sanitary districts. Things had been so bad in Manchester that James Nasmyth chose Patricroft as the location for his engineering works. The death-rate there was only a third of Manchester's; Nasmyth wrote that Patricroft offered his workers 'the benefit of breathing pure air during the greater part of the year'. But Nasmyth was no fool. He was one of a growing number of industrialists who had realised that a healthy workforce was an efficient workforce, and an efficient workforce contributed to the profitability of the company; therefore everyone gained. Nasmyth, like the Grants of Ramsbottom, was a Scot, and most of the key posts at his works were filled by Scots. And though Nasmyth had a care for the health of his workers, he could not abide strikes, and would not hesitate to use strike-breakers to keep his works running.

Between 1850 and 1890 there was a steady decline in infectious diseases such as cholera and typhoid, thanks to improved water supplies, However, the disposal of sewage would remain a problem until well into the 20th century. In 1876 Wigan still had no uniform system of sewage disposal, though years before it had been said to be 'a compound of villainous smells'. Things were, in fact, little better in Manchester itself. It was not until the 1890s that the city began to get to grips with the problem, and even by 1902 the luxury of flush lavatories applied to only 37 per cent of the city. In the older run-down areas of tenements, back-to-back houses, basement rooms, and back courts, ashpits and pail closets were the norm. The pail closets were nicknamed 'Dolly Vardens' after a perfume of the day. On the other hand, the good people of Sale were only too pleased to show off their sewage works. Commissioned in 1892 at a cost of £18,000, it could treat up to 750,000 gallons of sewage a day before pumping it into the Mersey, though some of the costs were recovered with the sale of the sludge to farmers.

The 1887 visit coincided with the Royal Exhibition. The 1894 and 1895 visits were primarily to photograph the Manchester Ship Canal throughout its length; within the archive there are pictures of Eastham Locks, Runcorn, Latchford Locks, Barton Swing Aqueduct, and Manchester Docks. Officially opened by Queen Victoria in 1894, the port of Manchester was an instant success; by 1900 annual exports were in excess of one million tonnes, rising to over 2.3 million tonnes annually by the end of 1907. In 1902 the port attracted business from Elders & Fyffes, and for a few years Manchester was the country's

principal port for the import of bananas. As with all the places they photographed, Frith cameramen continued to visit at regular intervals over the years. Our latest pictures of the MSC date from c1965, about three years before the container terminal was opened on the north end of No9 Dock. It was the withdrawal of this traffic that spelt the end for the port, though it has subsequently been redeveloped for residential, leisure, and commercial uses.

The final section includes the parts of Cheshire absorbed into the Greater Manchester Metropolitan County. Over the years Cheshire has undergone a number of changes to its boundaries. In 1931 Manchester was allowed to annex Northenden, Northen Etchells and Baguley, and five years later Taxal was transferred to Derbyshire, though Ludworth and Mellor were handed over in exchange. In 1974 the

metropolitan areas of Manchester and Merseyside effectively robbed Cheshire of much of its territory in the north-east and north-west of the county. Gone was the whole of the Wirral, together with Stalybridge, Sale, Altrincham, Bowdon and Langdendale: the latter was given to Derbyshire.

The towns of Altrincham and Bowdon were photographed in 1889, 1892, 1897, 1900, 1903, 1907, and 1913, but we have no picture of Cheadle before about 1955. Bowdon, along with Lymm, was the only place in north Cheshire where the Domesday Book records the presence of a church. The parish church dedicated to St Mary appears in several of the Bowdon pictures. The present structure has some 14th-century features, including a monument to a knight of the Baguley family. The church itself was rebuilt between 1858 and 1860 to the designs of W H Brakespeare, who was also responsible for St Paul's Church, Enville Road. Bowdon's popularity as a residential area for wealthy Mancunians grew in the 1850s and 1860s following the opening of the railway. The church at Cheadle features in a picture taken c1960. It was a place noted for absentee rectors, one of whom was Edward Trafford, who took himself off to Italy for his health; another rector only managed to put in six months' work out of an eight-year period 'due to stress'. Then there was the sexton who, saddened at the loss of fees because funerals were going to other places, regularly sought comfort and consolation in the nearby tavern. Every night the sexton had to leave the tavern and return to the church to ring the curfew bell. One night, a sweep climbed up into the belfry and rigged the bell so that it would not ring. Then he lay in wait. Presently our inebriated sexton

arrived. The bell made no sound. Suddenly the sexton heard a voice crying 'Thomas, my son, Thomas, my son!' He looked up, but all he could see in the gloom was a pair of eyes staring back at him. The sexton rushed out of the church shouting 'Murther, murther, the devil's put me shoulder out!'

Of all the Cheshire towns to be absorbed into Greater Manchester the most important is, of course, Stockport. Its name derives from the Saxon for a fortified or stockaded place in the woods. The town received its first charter in 1220 when it was made a free borough by Sir Robert de Stockport; a second charter in 1260 granted a weekly market and an annual fair to be held on the feast of St Wilfred. A castle existed here in the late 12th century, though the last traces of it were swept away around 1775. By far the largest of the Cheshire towns, it had a population of 22,000 in 1801 which had risen to 93,000 by 1901; at this time, the population of Manchester stood at 544,000, Salford at 220,000, and Bolton at 168,000. Our photograph features Little Under Bank and the premises of Winter's jewellery shop. Jacob Winter moved to Little Under Bank in about 1880. A security-conscious soul, Winter had the contents of his shop windows displayed on a hydraulic stage system powered by natural spring water that could be lowered into the cellar. The shop, as with many along this street, was built into the rock face and does not have a rear entrance.

This book is not an academic history of Greater Manchester, but we hope that the introduction and the captions that accompany our photographs take you on an interesting and occasionally surprising journey round the area.

URMSTON, CROFTS BANK ROAD c1950 U23002
Urmston is noted for being the birthplace in 1708 of John Collier, Lancashire's first dialect poet. It also has three Jewish cemeteries: one for the New Synagogue, one for the Polish Jews, and one for the Spanish and Portuguese Synagogue.

BARTON-UPON-IRWELL, BARTON AQUEDUCT 1894 33693
The unique Barton Swing Aqueduct was designed by Edward Leader Williams to carry the Bridgewater Canal over the Manchester Ship Canal. The requirement was that the aqueduct had to be capable of being swung clear whilst full of water, so as not to interfere with shipping movements on the MSC. The canal tow-path across the aqueduct is the raised platform on the left.

BARTON-UPON-IRWELL, BARTON BRIDGE 1894 33691
Both the 800-tonne Swing Aqueduct and the swing road bridge have been opened to allow the passage of a steamer on the MSC. Normal operating practice is for the bridge and aqueduct to be swung clear of the MSC approximately 30 minutes before a ship is due to pass through. The reason is that in the event of a failure of the opening mechanisms, there would be time to bring the ship to a halt.

BARTON-UPON-IRWELL, BARTON BRIDGE c1955 B781025
Barton Bridge closed in favour of road traffic. By the early 1950s, exports from Manchester Docks fluctuated at between 4 million and 5 million tonnes a year, while imports varied greatly, with 1959 being the bumper year at 13.5 million tonnes. Raw cotton imports and finished cotton exports represented about 70 per cent of the value of goods being shipped, though since 1951 oil had become the primary tonnage commodity.

PATRICROFT

Liverpool Road c1955 P158003

It was the opening of James Nasmyth's engineering works that
led to the growth of Eccles and Patricroft. Nasmyth chose
Patricroft because of 'the benefit of breathing pure air during
the greater part of the year'; being no fool, he was one of many
industrialists who had grasped the fact that a healthy workforce
is a more efficient workforce. Nasmyth's manufactured steam
hammers; one even appears on the armorial bearings of the
borough. They later developed the steam-powered pile-driver as
well as building railway locomotives. Other industries included
coal mines, a silk mill, a magnesium works, and a mining
equipment manufacturer.

ECCLES, THE TOWN HALL c1955 E88007
The Town Hall, in Church Street, was designed by John Lowe and erected during 1880-81 on the site of the old cockpit. A charter of incorporation was granted in 1892: the borough was formed out of Barton, Eccles, Winton, and Monton.

ECCLES, THE MONUMENT c1955 E88013
Here we see the town's monument to the memory of those from Eccles who gave their lives during two world wars. To the left is the public library, designed by Edward Potts and noted for its Venetian windows.

ECCLES, THE BROADWAY CINEMA c1955 E88020
The Associated British Cinema's picture house is photographed at a time when such places had fewer things to compete with for people's time and money; private car ownership was still beyond most people, television was in its infancy, and bingo halls, bowling alleys, shopping malls, videos, computers, package holidays and so on were in the future.

WORSLEY, THE COURT HOUSE 1889 22267
The impressive-looking Court House appears to be 16th-century, but it was in fact erected in 1849.

WORSLEY, THE CHURCH 1889 22265
Dedicated to St Mark, the church was designed by George Gilbert Scott and built in 1846. It is noted for the many gargoyles that festoon its tower, while inside there is a monument to the First Earl of Ellesmere.

WORSLEY, OLD HALL 1889 22161

The former seat of the Earl of Ellesmere, Worsley Old Hall dates from the 16th century. It was here that James Brindley lived while working on the Bridgewater Canal. It was also the residence of the Duke's agent John Gilbert, who is thought to have played a major role in the design of the underground canal network used to bring coal out of his grace's mines.

WORSLEY, THE DELPH 1896 37432

This view looks towards one of the entrances to the series of underground canals that extended to the Duke's pits at Walkden. The boats at Delph were 50ft long, 6ft 4in wide, 7ft beam and drew 2ft 10in when laden. At Worsley the boats were lashed together in threes, and three such groups were then towed behind a pair of horses to Manchester. The journey took about five hours, and each delivered between 90 and 100 tonnes of coal.

WORSLEY, THE WOODEN BRIDGE c1955 W145054

The wooden bridge spans the spur to the Delph. Here, iron ore deposits colour the water bright orange. There were two canal and tunnel systems, one set higher than the other. Linked by an inclined plane on a 1 in 4 gradient, the boats were carried between levels on a rail-mounted cradle. A series of sluices helped create a slight current of about half-a-mile an hour, which was enough to carry the loaded boats out into the Delph.

WORSLEY, THE PACKET HOUSE 1889 22262

The Packet House was a scheduled stop for passenger boats plying the Bridgewater Canal. There were different types of craft employed; the basic packet on the Warrington-Manchester run carried passengers at 1s a head. The packet service from Manchester to Liverpool via Worsley, Leigh and Wigan took fourteen hours, though meals were provided at 1s each.

SWINTON, THE CHURCH 1896 37423
Swinton and Pendlebury lie to the north-west of Salford. St Peter's is the only church in the Manchester area to have been commissioned from George Edmund Street. The project was plagued with a lack of money from the start, and Street had to redraw the plans and cut costs. The lack of a clerestory makes the nave very dark.

LEIGH, MARKET STREET 1950 L325002
Leigh was a market town that prospered on coal, cotton, and silk. It is also the last resting place of Sir Thomas Tyldesley, who had accompanied the Earl of Derby's 1651 invasion of Lancashire from the Isle of Man in support of Charles II. Derby had expected to join up with the King at Wigan, but instead clashed with and was routed by Robert Lilburne's Parliamentarian troops. The Earl was with the King at the Battle of Worcester, but was later captured and executed at Bolton. He his buried in the family vault at Ormskirk.

ATHERTON, MARKET STREET C1955 A138008

In July 1889 Walter Davies, manager of a pawnshop in Market Street, was found dying from a stab wound to his neck. The murderer William Chadwick was tracked down and eventually stood trial at Liverpool Assizes. He was hanged in April 1890. Dominating our picture is St Michael's Church, which dates from about 1400, though it was extensively rebuilt between 1840 and 1844; the tower received similar treatment during 1886-88.

ATHERTON, STREET SCENE C1960 A138017

Atherton was a cotton-spinning town, and for 200 years a mining community. Local collieries included Howe Bridge, Gibfield, and Chanter. Howe Bridge was closed by the NCB in 1957; Gibfield followed in 1963, and Chanter in 1966.

WESTHOUGHTON
Market Street c1955 W250001
On the northern edge of the Wigan coalfield, local pits once
provided employment for over 2000 miners, but by the late
1940s the mines were just a memory. At various times
Westhoughton has been home to Metal Box, the Houghton
Weavers, and rice pudding with a crust on the top, as well as
being one of the last bastions of the Pasty Feast. This latter
festivity involved local pubs turning out a variety of home-made
pasties. The finder of a small pot doll in his pasty was not only
blessed with good luck, but he was also expected
to buy a round.

WIGAN, GENERAL VIEW C1960 W985001
Standing in the upper Douglas Valley, Wigan was once a market town, but by the mid 19th century it was a major centre for Lancashire's coal industry. Times change, however, and by the 1960s the town was almost ringed with derelict pits, spoil heaps, and scars from the ravages of open cast workings.

WIGAN, THE PARISH CHURCH 1895 36810
All Saints was virtually rebuilt during the late 1840s. The west tower was heightened in 1861, but the lower part is 13th-century, or perhaps even earlier, as the walls here are 6ft thick and there is also a garderobe chamber. In the church there is a monument to Sir William Bradshaigh and his wife.

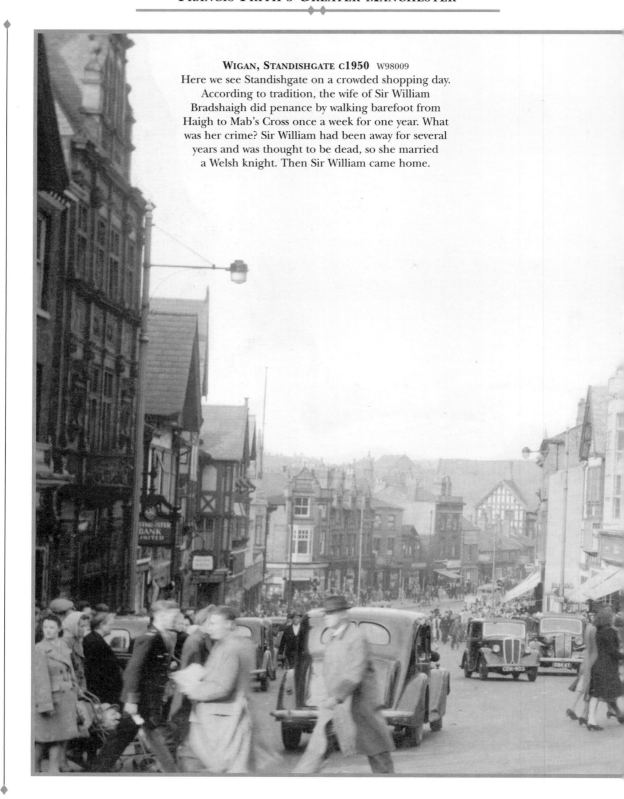

WIGAN, STANDISHGATE c1950 W98009
Here we see Standishgate on a crowded shopping day.
According to tradition, the wife of Sir William
Bradshaigh did penance by walking barefoot from
Haigh to Mab's Cross once a week for one year. What
was her crime? Sir William had been away for several
years and was thought to be dead, so she married
a Welsh knight. Then Sir William came home.

WIGAN, THE INFIRMARY 1896 37397

By 1896 Wigan was taking public health seriously, and not only in the provision of hospital beds. In 1868 Manchester and Liverpool were the only Lancashire authorities with medical officers of health, and as late as 1876 Wigan still lacked a uniform system for disposing of or treating sewage. The place was said to be 'a compound of villainous smells'.

WIGAN, HAIGH HALL 1896 37400

Haigh Hall was designed by the twenty-fourth Earl of Crawford for himself and built at a cost of £100,000 between c1832 and 1840. Stone for the building was cut on site by machinery brought to the estate by way of the Leeds & Liverpool Canal. The timber came from the Haigh and from Crawford's estates in Jamaica.

WIGAN
Haigh Park Entrance 1895
The arched gate and the lodges at the entrance to Haigh Park are thought to date from c1840. The 200-acre estate was acquired by the corporation in 1947; the hall now houses a local history museum, and is also used for exhibitions.

◆

BOLTON
Smithill's Hall 1894
Smithill's Hall occupies a site where, according to tradition, a chapel dedicated to the Blessed Virgin was consecrated in AD793 and the wandering court of King Egbert, father of Alfred the Great, was entertained. The Hall dates from the 15th century, when it was the home of the Radcliffe family, though a later occupier, Andrew Barton, extended it in about 1516. It was bought by Bolton Corporation in 1933.

WIGAN, HAIGH PARK ENTRANCE 1895 36816

BOLTON, SMITHILL'S HALL 1894 34392

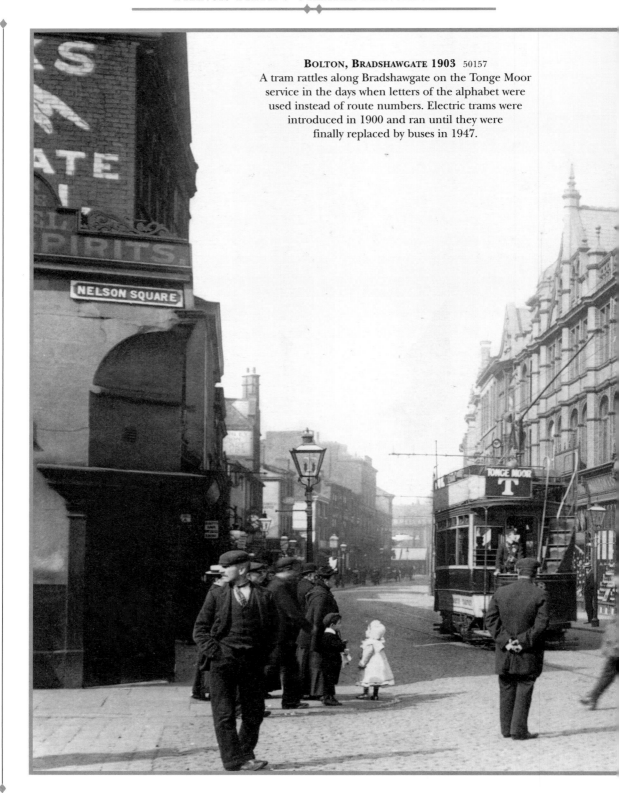

BOLTON, BRADSHAWGATE 1903 50157
A tram rattles along Bradshawgate on the Tonge Moor service in the days when letters of the alphabet were used instead of route numbers. Electric trams were introduced in 1900 and ran until they were finally replaced by buses in 1947.

NELSON SQUARE

BOLTON, THE TOWN HALL 1893 33067

One of the lasting impressions of Bolton that many a visitor has is of the grand Town Hall, with its portico of Corinthian columns and tower topped off with a French cap. A classic building in more ways than one, it was designed by William Hill, erected between 1867 and 1873, and extended in the early 1930s.

BOLTON, NELSON SQUARE 1893 33073

This view was taken from the Infirmary end of the square, looking towards the junction with Bradshawgate. The large building at centre left is the post office, and just in front of that and to the right of James Wilde & Son is the single-storey Pack Horse Hotel.

BOLTON
Deansgate 1895 35850
In the 1890s Deansgate was one of the
main shopping streets and commercial
districts. On the left is the imposing bulk
of William Deacon's Bank; also along
here was the Bank of Bolton, which was
later taken over by Barclay's.

BOLTON, ST PETER'S CHURCH, HALLIWELL 1898 40108
St Peter's is the earliest of the churches in Halliwell. When it was erected in 1840, it comprised a one-bay chancel and no aisles. Other places of worship in Halliwell were St Paul's (1847), St Luke's (1869-75), St Thomas's (1875) and St Margaret's (1903).

TOTTINGTON, GENERAL VIEW c1955 T144004
The manor or honour of Tottington covered 15 square miles, and was awarded to General George Monck (1608-70) for services to the Crown. A former Royalist officer who changed sides after being captured, Monck fought with distinction on the side of Parliament. A firm believer in the authority of civil power, he was instrumental in securing the restoration of Charles II following the collapse of Richard Cromwell's protectorate. Monck was later created First Duke of Albermarle.

TOTTINGTON
Market Street c1955

Tottington's unusual claim to fame is that it is one of the most northerly places to have suffered a hit from a German V1 flying bomb, or Doodlebug, during the Second World War.

The weapon was air-launched on 24 December 1944 from under the wing of a bomber; this was at best a somewhat dangerous procedure, even for the aircrew. It landed on a row of cottages in Chapel Street opposite St Anne's Church, killing seven residents. The event is commemorated by the Whitehead Garden.

BURY
Walshaw Church 1895

Situated on a hill overlooking the town, Christ Church, or the Jesse Haworth Memorial Church, was designed by Lawrence Booth and built in the late 1880s. A large church with fine Gothic windows, it was paid for by the Haworth family, who had made their money from cotton spinning and fustian making.

TOTTINGTON, MARKET STREET c1955 T144002

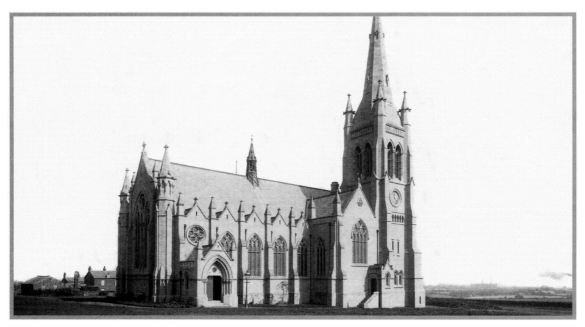

BURY, WALSHAW CHURCH 1895 36807

BURY, THE TOWN HALL AND CLOCK TOWER c1955 B257014

Though built of quality stone, the Town Hall, designed by Reginald Edmunds in the 1930s, has little in the way of decoration; in that respect it is eclipsed by the ornate clock tower erected to the memory of Walter Whitehead. Born in Bury in 1840, Walter was appointed to the surgical staff of Manchester Royal Infirmary in 1873 and went on to become one of the most brilliant surgeons of his time.

BURY, THE MARKET 1902 48562

The Earl of Derby both gave the land and also paid for the construction of the market, which opened in 1841. In those days it was open to the elements; in 1867 it was decided that it should be covered over with an iron and glass roof. The alterations were designed by a Mr Green, who was the Earl's architect at Redvales. The market re-opened in April 1868; the alterations cost about £5000.

BURY, MARKET PLACE 1895 36783
A church existed on this site at the time of William the Conqueror, and the Domesday survey lists its patron as Roger de Poictou. The church of St Mary, which stood here in c1773, was demolished except for its tower and spire, and then rebuilt. In 1843 the tower and spire were dismantled, and subsequently rebuilt during 1844-45. By 1869-70 the body of the church was found to be suffering from wood rot and was declared unsafe. Demolition began in 1870, but once again the tower and spire were spared. A new chancel and nave were erected between 1872 and 1876.

BURY, MARKET PLACE c1955 B257019
About sixty years separate this view and photograph No 36783. During that time, the horse has given way to the internal combustion engine; trams have been and gone; the statue of Sir Robert Peel now stands guard over a gents' toilet; and a memorial commemorates Bury's suffering during the insanity of two world wars.

BURY, FLEET STREET 1895 36779
It was from the Old Boar's Head in Fleet Street that
travellers could take a coach to Colne or Manchester.
The town's other coaching inns were the Grey Mare Inn
in the Market Place for services to Leeds, York, Liverpool,
Manchester and Clitheroe; the Eagle & Child in Silver
Street for Manchester and Skipton via Burnley and
Colne; and the White Lion in Millgate for Manchester.

BURY, THE TECHNICAL SCHOOL 1895 36792

Designed by Maxwell & Tuke and completed in 1894, the Technical School, Broad Street, was built to fulfil the requirements of the Technical Instruction Act (1890). Technical education had received a boost during the 1880s when towns like Bradford committed funds to build specialist colleges. They believed such places were essential if their industry was to keep abreast of foreign competition and innovation.

BURY, WALMERSLEY CHURCH 1897 40107

Walmersley was a township within Bury on the east bank of the Irwell. Christ Church was erected in 1838 and comprised a chancel, nave and a low tower, but it was soon replaced by a new building designed by Maxwell & Tuke. John Robinson Kay, born in Burnley in July 1805, died at Walmersley House in March 1872. He held directorships with the Lancashire & Yorkshire Railway, the Manchester & County Bank, and the Thames & Mersey Insurance Co, but is remembered for his active role in winning shorter factory working hours for women and children.

BURY, HOLCOMBE HILL 1896 37390
One of the principal roads from the south into the Forest of Rossendale was from Bury to Clitheroe, the route skirting the edge of Holcombe Hill and Haslingden. The Peel Tower on Holcombe Hill was erected in 1852 to the memory of Sir Robert Peel.

RAMSBOTTOM, VIEW OF THE TOWN c1955 R253017
Ramsbottom is a small cotton town on the Irwell less than four miles north of Bury, and just over eleven miles from Manchester. It is noted for its surrounding countryside: to the west rises Harcles Hill (1216 ft), while over to the east stands Whittle Hill (1534 ft). Local businessmen William and Daniel Grant were the basis for the Cheeryble brothers in Charles Dickens' masterpiece 'Nicholas Nickleby'.

RAMSBOTTOM, VIEW OF THE TOWN c1955 R253015
In the last quarter of the 18th century Ramsbottom was a hamlet of perhaps no more than six or seven cottages. It was the plentiful water supply which attracted industry, providing power for spinning mills and bleaching and dye works.

HEYWOOD, THE CENTRE c1955 H228010

HEYWOOD
The Centre c1955

St Luke's is Heywood's oldest place of worship, and is known to have existed prior to 1611. It was rebuilt between 1860 and 1862 to the design of Joseph Clarke; Yorkshire parpoint and Staffordshire ashlar were used for the external work and Bath stone ashlar inside. The detached tower and spire stands 188ft high; also featured in this picture is the large west window.

HEALEY DELL 1898

Judging by the debris and the description of its location on a bend of the river, this is where the water-powered mill used to be situated.

HEALEY DELL 1898 41031

HEALEY DELL, THE VIADUCT 1895 36767

HEALEY DELL, THE FAIRY CHAPEL 1913 65608

HEALEY DELL
The Viaduct 1895

This once thickly-wooded dell on both sides of the River Spodden had been thinned out somewhat by the 1890s. Byron brought his distant kinswoman Mary Ann Chaworth, with whom he was in love, here when they visited Rochdale and were staying as the guests of Thomas Fferrand.

◆

HEALEY DELL
The Fairy Chapel 1913

The chapel was in fact little more than a recess in the rock face. Of the fairies, Fferrand wrote: 'amongst the uneducated people in Rochdale the superstition of fairies has not been dispelled, and Shakespeare, Drayton, and other poets, in the exercise of their poetical fancy, have given these airy beautiful miniature human beings an existence'.

ROCHDALE
John Bright's Statue 1898

Following the death of his wife Elizabeth from tuberculosis, John Bright's world was in shreds. Then along came Alderman Richard Cobden. It was he who brought purpose back into Bright's life when he reminded him that hundreds of people were dying of starvation due to the iniquitous Corn Laws. Bright and Cobden became a formidable team, for they worked well together, and the Corn Laws were repealed by Sir Robert Peel in 1846.

◆

ROCHDALE
Church Steps 1913

This flight of 122 steps leads up to the parish church dedicated to St Chad. A local legend says that the church was to have been built on the banks of the River Roch, but every night the materials were mysteriously shifted to the top of a nearby hill by 'goblin builders'.

ROCHDALE, JOHN BRIGHT'S STATUE 1898 41022

ROCHDALE, CHURCH STEPS 1913 65603

ROCHDALE, THE TOWN HALL 1892 30397
The Town Hall was designed by the Leeds architect W H Crossland in a Gothic Flemish style and built between 1866 and 1871. The building is 303 ft long; the Great Hall is 90 ft long, and is noted for its fine mosaic floors.

ROCHDALE, TOWN HALL SQUARE 1892 30396
The Square is dominated by the 190ft-high Town Hall tower. Even in 1892 it was not the original; that had been so badly damaged by fire that it had to be demolished. Its replacement was designed by Alfred Waterhouse and built in 1883. In the background is the parish church of St Chad's.

ROCHDALE
Entrance to Yorkshire Street 1898 41023
Yorkshire Street was one of the main shopping streets in the town. Along here could be found McDonnell's store, which was the place to go for fresh Irish eggs and home-cured Irish ham. Then there was the shop of Harvey Pearse, bookseller and stationer; John Hurst the music seller, pianoforte and harmonium dealer; Williamson's the jewellers and silversmiths; and F C Greenwood, boot and shoe maker.

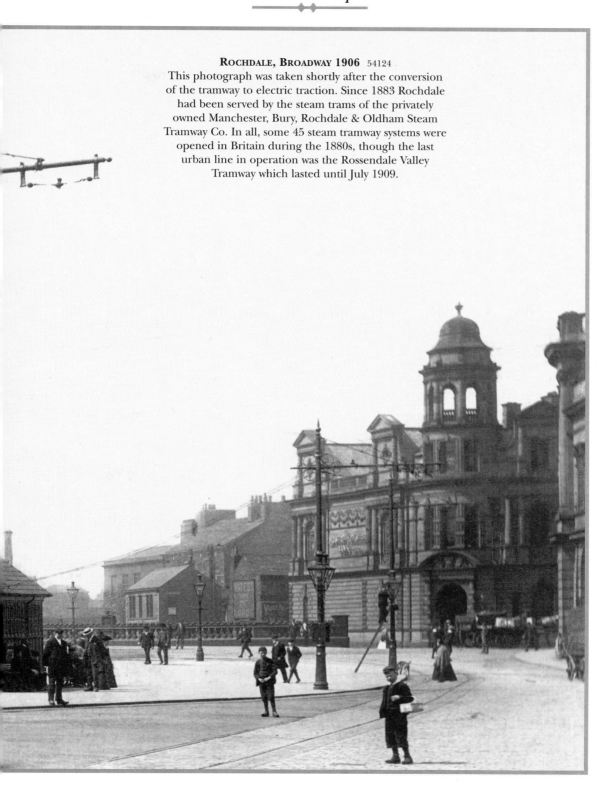

ROCHDALE, BROADWAY 1906 54124
This photograph was taken shortly after the conversion
of the tramway to electric traction. Since 1883 Rochdale
had been served by the steam trams of the privately
owned Manchester, Bury, Rochdale & Oldham Steam
Tramway Co. In all, some 45 steam tramway systems were
opened in Britain during the 1880s, though the last
urban line in operation was the Rossendale Valley
Tramway which lasted until July 1909.

ROCHDALE, BROADWAY 1913 30397A
Intending passengers await the arrival of their tram.
Rochdale abandoned its tramway system in November
1932; it was a casualty of the Depression, along with
many of the town's cotton mills. With so many towns-
folk out of work, revenue plummeted, and there was
little alternative but to replace the trams with more
economical, and from an operating point
of view, more flexible buses.

ROCHDALE, THE ESPLANADE 1902 48575

The antics of our cameraman has attracted the attention of a number of boys gathered round the white marble angel that stands in front of the gates to Hillside Gardens. In the gardens, and to the left of the statue, stands the obelisk erected to the memory of the town's dialect poets Margaret Lahee, Oliver Ormerod, Edwin Waugh, and John Trafford Clegg.

ROCHDALE, VIEW FROM THE SLOPE 1913 65604

This picture fits the description of Rochdale that appears in the 1906 Baedecker guide: 'a town of over 90,000 inhab., situated on the Roche, and is one of the chief seats of the flannel and woollen industry and has also many large cotton-mills'.

ROCHDALE, HOLLINGWORTH LAKE 1892 30401A
Hollingworth Lake was originally constructed as a feeder for the Rochdale Canal. Completed in 1804, this 33 mile-long canal linked the Bridgewater Canal to the Calder & Hebble Navigation, and was one of three trans-Pennine waterways. Apart from the section between Castlefields and Dale Street Basin in Manchester, the canal was abandoned in 1952, and Hollingworth Lake was finally given over to recreation and leisure activities.

ROCHDALE, HOLLINGWORTH LAKE 1895 36777

With a water surface of ninety acres and surrounded by open spaces, Hollingworth Lake became a popular destination for workers on their days off. At one time it was a favourite venue for gala days and brass band competitions, with special trains bringing people from such places as Leeds, Bradford, Bury and Oldham.

LITTLEBOROUGH, HOLLINGWORTH LAKE c1955 L182006

Here we see the harbour on Hollingworth Lake. Not only were rowing boats, racing skiffs and dinghies a common sight, but there was even a time when the lake had its own paddle steamer. As can be seen in photograph 36777, Hollingworth supported a number of hotels, one of which, the Beach, featured refreshment rooms that overhung the water and a dancing stage for 2,000 people. Another hotel, The Lake, was designed in the Swiss Chalet style.

LITTLEBOROUGH, HOLLINGWORTH LAKE c1960 L182010
This view shows Hollingworth on a glorious summer's day, with both the paddle boats and the ice cream vans doing brisk trade.

CHADDERTON, THE LIBRARY c1955 C284004
Only a few years before this picture was taken, a Chadderton factory was making a vital contribution to the war effort. Having been bombed out of their works at Mitcham, Surrey, A C Cossor Ltd were relocated to Chadderton; they were housed in the old Wren Mill which had been converted into a government Shadow factory. Cossors manufactured 'Gee' equipment for aircraft, which detected signals from Loran (long range air navigation) transmitters. This device enabled the navigator of a long range bomber to plot his aircraft's position quickly and accurately.

DELPH, ROSEHILL c1955 D105014

In the early decades of the 19th century the district of Saddleworth covered 35 square miles and included over 70 hamlets and villages. Though within the parish of Rochdale, Saddleworth lay in the extreme south-west of the West Riding of Yorkshire and was long talked of as the part of Yorkshire where Lancastrians lived.

DELPH, THE BRIDGE c1955 D105001

As well as being in the West Riding, Saddleworth was also in the wapentake of Agbrigg. Wapentake literally means 'show of weapons', and was the old Danish way of voting. All those eligible would attend an open-air meeting where they would discuss and then vote on laws, or make resolutions, by raising their swords, axes or spears. The district is also divided into four meres, an old term for boundary, comprising Quickmere, Shawmere, Lordsmere, and Friarsmere; they come together at Delph.

DELPH, KING STREET c1955 D105010

Delph and Dobcross were two of the principal villages within Saddleworth. In the 1820s Dobcross possessed two banks (Buckley & Co and Harrop & Co), while Delph supported an agent for the Genuine Tea Co (John Brook), an attorney (Jonas Ainley), and an auctioneer (Timothy Bradbury), together with a baker, blacksmith, coal merchant, and at least four boot and shoe makers.

DELPH, TAMEWATER FROM STONESWOOD ROAD c1955 D105008

In the 1820s Tame Water was described as 'a small hamlet near Dobcross'. In those days the Harrop family appear to have played a major role in the industry of the hamlet; there was James Harrop & Sons, drysalters and oil dealers, and Harrop Booth & Co, woollen cloth manufacturers.

DELPH, HEYS c1955 D105025

Writing in 1822, Edward Baines said of the area that 'on the whole, Saddleworth is an interesting, though an uninviting part of the country, and the Mountaineers of this region, like those of Switzerland, have a character peculiar to themselves: they are rude of speech, but kind and hospitable in disposition, without many benefits of education, but quick of perception and sound judgement'.

SALFORD, PEEL PARK MUSEUM 1889 22164

Peel Park opened in 1846 and is named in honour of Prime Minister Sir Robert Peel. He not only secured government funding for the park, but made a generous donation himself. To the right of the statue is Lark Hill, a mansion built in 1790 and formerly the home of Colonel Ackers of the Manchester & Salford Volunteers. In January 1850 Lark Hill became Britain's first totally free public library. The original house was demolished in 1937.

SALFORD, PEEL PARK 1889 22167

Peel Park was somewhere Salfordians could go and seek refuge for a few hours from the noise, muck, and drudgery of day-to-day living. In those days the main entrance to the park had an ornate arch, Brighton Pavilion meets the Taj Mahal in style, erected to commemorate Queen Victoria's visit of 1857. It was declared unsafe and demolished in July 1937.

MANCHESTER, THE DOCKS c1965 M21503
This view looks along No9 Dock looking towards No 2 Grain Elevator. The withdrawal
of container traffic spelt the end for Manchester, and by the early 1980s the docks had
been flattened in readiness for redevelopment, both for residential and leisure purposes.

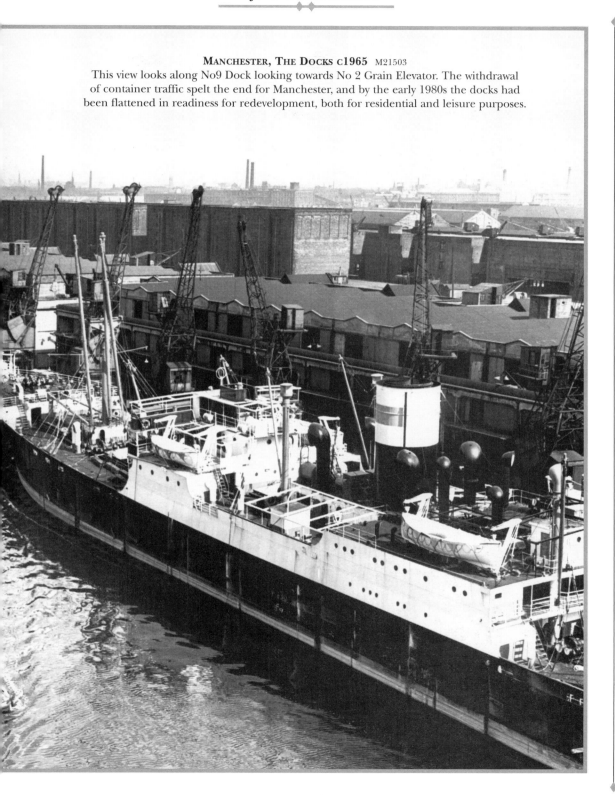

MANCHESTER, THE DOCKS 1895 36387

Though called Manchester Docks, most of the port was in fact in Salford; only the Pomona wharfs, which handled coastal vessels and short sea routes, were in Manchester. Here we see numbers 6, 7 and 8 Docks, built for handling ocean-going ships. In 1902 Elders & Fyffes in association with the United Fruit Co moved their operations to Manchester, with the result that for a few years it was the country's leading banana port.

MANCHESTER, THE DOCKS c1965 M21502

This photograph was taken several years before the opening of the container terminal on North No 9 Dock. Containerization traffic led Manchester Liners to restructure their fleet. Some ships, such as 'Manchester Progress' (8176 grt), were converted to cellular containerships, and new ships were ordered, such as 'Manchester Challenge' (12,000 grt) and her sisters 'Manchester Courage' and 'Manchester Concorde'.

MANCHESTER
From the Victoria Hotel 1889 21884

Over on the left is Manchester Exchange station, opened by the
London & North Western Railway in 1884 and famous for the
long platform which linked it to Victoria Station. On the right
is the tower of the cathedral, which was rebuilt between 1864
and 1867; the remainder of the cathedral was heavily restored
during the 1880s. The statue of Oliver Cromwell by Matthew
Noble was a gift to the city by Mrs Abel Heywood in memory
of her first husband. Apparently Manchester was divided over
whether or not to accept it. It was the first large-scale statue
of Cromwell to be raised in the open anywhere in England.

MANCHESTER, DEANSGATE 1892 30384
The triangular-shaped Victoria Buildings was erected by
the corporation in 1876 occupying an area of land
bounded by Deansgate, Victoria Street, and St Mary's Gate.
The corporation laid a circuit of tracks around the
building which in-bound trams followed. This did away
with the need to turn the trams, for by completing the
circuit they would automatically be facing in the right
direction for their next outward trip.

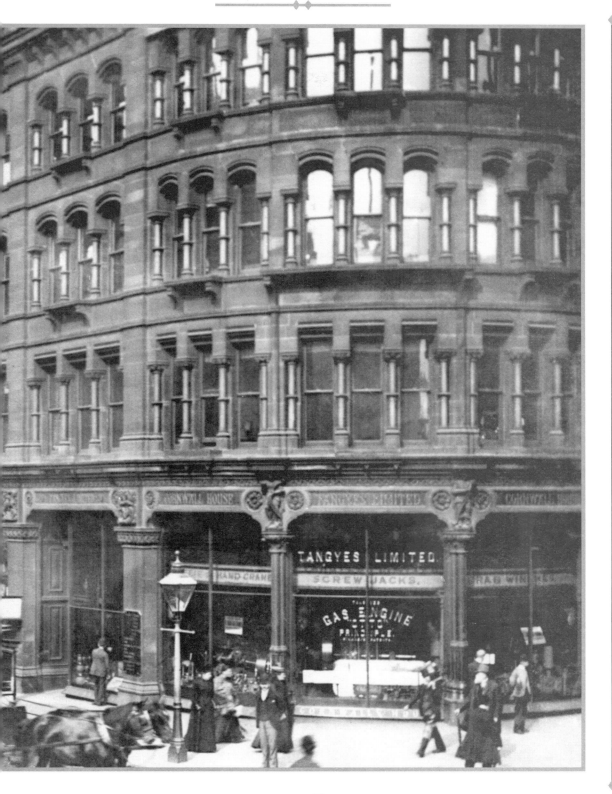

MANCHESTER, THE CATHEDRAL 1889 21870
Dedicated to the Glorious Virgin and the holy martyrs St Denis and St George, the cathedral was originally built as a collegiate church by Thomas, Lord de la Warre, in the 15th century. It was the church's first warden, John Huntington, who built the choir; his successor added the nave, and the third warden widened the choir and added the clerestory. During restoration work in the 1880s some fragments of Saxon masonry was unearthed.

MANCHESTER
Victoria Buildings Gateway c1876

When completed, the Victoria Buildings had 31 shops on the ground floor and numerous suites of offices above. Through the centre of the complex ran the Victoria Arcade, whilst at the Victoria Street/Deansgate end was the 100-room Victoria Hotel. The building was destroyed during an air raid in December 1940. The site was later incorporated into the Arndale Centre development.

◆

MANCHESTER
St Ann's Square 1886

Once known as Acres Field, it was here for about 500 years that Manchester's weekly markets and annual fairs were held. In 1709 the foundation stone of St Ann's was laid; the church was a gift to the town from Lady Ann Bland. It was completed in 1712, and by the mid 18th century St Ann's was the fashionable part of town, the place to see and be seen in.

MANCHESTER, VICTORIA BUILDINGS GATEWAY c1876 8288

MANCHESTER, ST ANN'S SQUARE 1886 18265

MANCHESTER, ST ANN'S SQUARE 1885 18263
This view looks towards the Royal Exchange and
St Mary's Gate. This was one of the principal cab ranks
in Manchester, and licensing, fares and conditions
were regulated by the local authority. Cabs could be
hired by time at 2s 6d per hour, or by distance, the
fare dependant upon the number of people sharing.

MANCHESTER, THE ROYAL EXCHANGE 1886 18259
The Royal Exchange was where the Lancashire cotton industry did business with the world. Covering 3699 square yards, the Exchange had accommodation for 6600 members when it was completed; it was opened in two phases, in 1871 and 1874.

MANCHESTER
The Royal Exchange 1885 18262
The floor of the Royal Exchange was the scene of frantic activity on Tuesdays and Fridays, when at the hour of High Exchange anything up to 6000 men would gather here and shout at one another. Though the floor appeared chaotic to the outsider, it was in fact well organised. Buyers, agents, manufacturers and merchants had their regular places. Those who did their business here would know where to find the Blackburn cotton manufacturers, or the Oldham cotton spinners, as well as cotton brokers, agents for the Indian and Chinese markets, and machinery manufacturers.

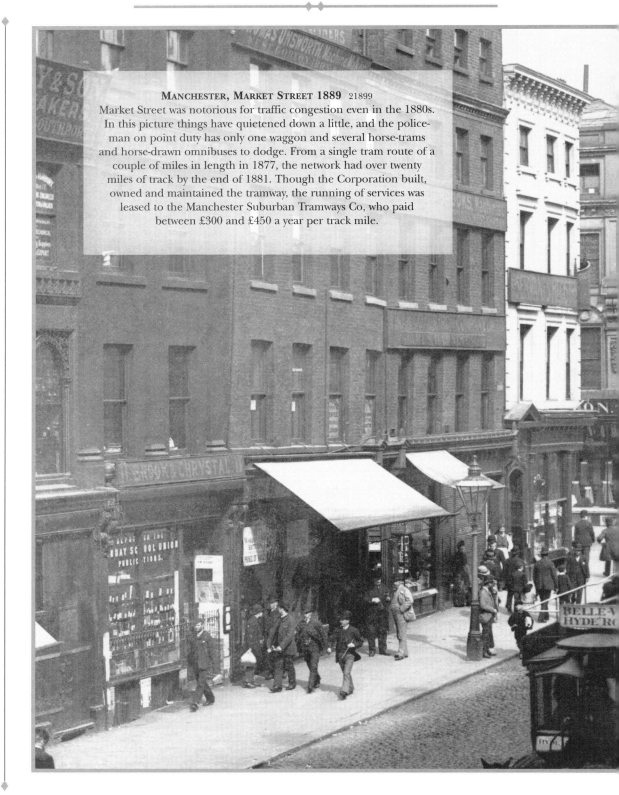

MANCHESTER, MARKET STREET 1889 21899
Market Street was notorious for traffic congestion even in the 1880s.
In this picture things have quietened down a little, and the police-
man on point duty has only one waggon and several horse-trams
and horse-drawn omnibuses to dodge. From a single tram route of a
couple of miles in length in 1877, the network had over twenty
miles of track by the end of 1881. Though the Corporation built,
owned and maintained the tramway, the running of services was
leased to the Manchester Suburban Tramways Co, who paid
between £300 and £450 a year per track mile.

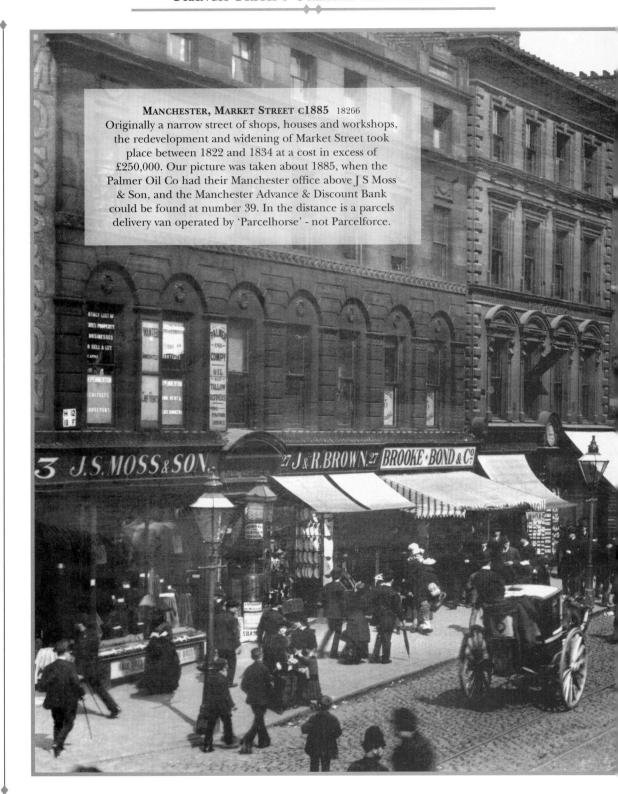

MANCHESTER, MARKET STREET c1885 18266
Originally a narrow street of shops, houses and workshops,
the redevelopment and widening of Market Street took
place between 1822 and 1834 at a cost in excess of
£250,000. Our picture was taken about 1885, when the
Palmer Oil Co had their Manchester office above J S Moss
& Son, and the Manchester Advance & Discount Bank
could be found at number 39. In the distance is a parcels
delivery van operated by 'Parcelhorse' - not Parcelforce.

MANCHESTER, MARKET STREET 1886 18270
Just on the left of the picture is the entrance to Lewis's Department Store, the first large-scale retail outlet in Manchester. By adopting a strategy that combined aggressive advertising with special offers, discounts and sales on specific lines, Lewis's was an immediate success; shoppers came from miles around in search of a bargain. Lewis worked on the principle of low profit margin but high stock turn.

MANCHESTER, PORTLAND STREET 1885 18284

Browsers graze the bargain boxes outside Sutton's bookshop. Most of them appear to have arrived on bicycles, as there are a number of machines parked up. In the warehouse district, Portland Street in 1885 began on the south side of the infirmary and was used to link Oxford Street and Piccadilly by tramway.

MANCHESTER, THE TOWN HALL 1889 21896

In 1866 the Corporation decided that the design for the Town Hall should be by open competition, a normal 19th-century practice for civic buildings. There were 130 entries, the winner being Alfred Waterhouse. The Town Hall covered a site of nearly two acres; building began in 1868 and was completed in 1877 at a cost of about £1million.

MANCHESTER, THE ASSIZE COURT 1886 18251
Costing over £130,000 to build and opened in July 1864, the Assize Court was a blend of Early English and Victorian Gothic. Behind the courts was the county prison, housing 800 male and 600 female prisoners. The prison was for its day a state-of-the-art secure establishment, with wings radiating out from a central block.

MANCHESTER INFIRMARY C1885 18256
The public infirmary, with just twelve beds, was established in 1752 in a house in Withy Grove, but was replaced by a 80-bed hospital in Piccadilly in 1755, where it remained for over 150 years. When this picture was taken, the infirmary had on its staff Walter Whitehead, probably one of the most talented surgeons of the late-Victorian era. Whitehead became famous for two procedures: one was the quick removal of a cancerous tongue using just a pair of scissors, the other was curing piles by what Walter referred to as 'excising the pile-bearing area'.

MANCHESTER, PICCADILLY 1887 22159
This photograph was taken from the Queen's Hotel
and looking across Piccadilly towards Market Street,
where we can see Lewis's Department Store. In the
foreground is a poster advertising the Royal Jubilee
Exhibition, which was opened by the Prince of Wales
and ran from May to October 1887.

MANCHESTER, ST PETER'S CHURCH c1885 18302

When it was completed in 1794, St Peter's Church was on the very edge of the built-up area of the town. St Peter's had a short career: it was demolished in 1907, and for a number of years its site was marked by a cross. After the Great War the site was chosen for the city's war memorial, which was designed by Lutyens and erected in 1924.

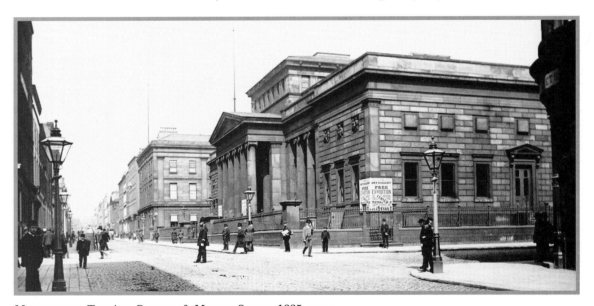

MANCHESTER, THE ART GALLERY & MOSLEY STREET 1885 18285

In 1824 the Royal Manchester Institution was hoping to move into a new headquarters in Mosley Street, and in the accepted practice of the day invited architects to submit their ideas by means of open competition. The winner was Charles Barry (1795-1860), who is best remembered for working in collaboration with Pugin on the designs for the House of Commons. The new building opened in 1834, but was taken over by Manchester Corporation in 1882 and became the City Art Gallery.

MANCHESTER, OWEN'S COLLEGE c1876 8295
The college was founded in 1845 by John Owen, who left £100,000 for the purpose. The college later moved into a new building on Oxford Road which had been designed by Alfred Waterhouse, winner of the competition to design Manchester Town Hall. The new college buildings were officially opened by the Duke of Devonshire in October 1873. The buildings pictured here are still extant; they are hidden from the main road by later buildings.

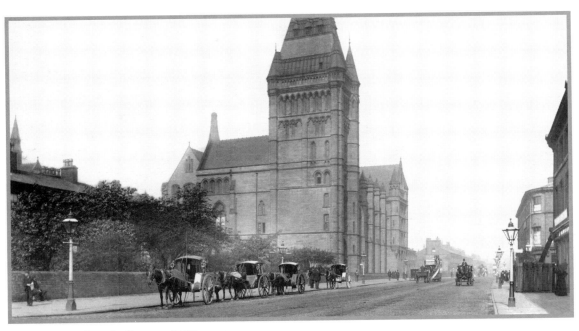

MANCHESTER, OWEN'S COLLEGE 1895 36350
As early as 1877 the Senate applied to the Privy Council for the college to be raised to a university, but the application was contested by similar institutions in Liverpool and Leeds. The outcome was the formation of the Victoria University. University College, Liverpool was admitted in 1884, and the Yorkshire College, Leeds in 1887.

**MANCHESTER, THE ROYAL JUBILEE EXHIBITION
ROYAL ENTRANCE 1887** 21901
The idea that the celebration of Queen Victoria's jubilee
should include an exhibition featuring Manchester's
business, commerce, and industry was first discussed in
1886. A 32-acre site adjoining the Botanical Gardens at
Old Trafford was chosen, as it had both rail and tramway
connections. Note the mock-up of the cathedral tower.

MANCHESTER, THE ROYAL JUBILEE EXHIBITION 1887 21903
Opened by the Prince of Wales on 3 May 1887, the exhibition ran for six months and attracted 4.75million visitors. The profit of £44,000 was handed over to the Whitworth Institute, who allocated £20,000 to establish a museum, £10,000 to develop a school of art, and £14,000 towards the new Technical School.

MANCHESTER, THE BLIND ASYLUM c1885 18307
As early as 1810 the town had been left a substantial amount of money (£20,000) towards an institution for the blind. Unfortunately, the benefactor Thomas Henshaw had stipulated in his will that the money had to be spent on things other than buildings; that was paid for by public subscription and completed in 1837.

DENTON, CROWN POINT c1955 D84001

By the time this picture was taken, the tram routes through Denton had been converted to trolley and petrol bus operations. The 1930s saw a number of towns and cities abandon tram routes in favour of trolleybuses; they were partially influenced by the findings of a Royal Commission on Transport. The Conran Street - Denton service was converted in December 1934, and the Ashton - Denton route in November 1936.

MELLOR, FROM COBDEN EDGE c1960 M157016

Straddling an unclassified road between Hayfield and Marple, the village of Mellor is noted for its church, which is dedicated to St Thomas. As can be seen from our picture, the church stands on an exposed hill above the village. Though rebuilt in the early 19th century, the church contains an early Norman drum-shaped font, and what is believed to be the oldest wooden pulpit in England.

ROMILEY

Compstall Road c1960 R255018

Even at this time Compstall Road, along with Stockport Road, had long been at the commercial heart of the town. At the beginning of the 20th century there were plenty of shops along Compstall Road, and it was also where Joseph Bullock had his saddlery business; the local police station had Harry Wibberley as constable in charge. One interesting fact about Romiley in the early 1900s was that the natives appear to have had a soft spot for confectionery; Kelly's Directory lists many sweet shops in this area.

STOCKPORT
Little Under Bank 1968

Our picture features Winter's jewellery shop and Petersgate Bridge. The bridge was built in 1868 to link the market square with St Petersgate. Jacob Winter moved his shop to Little Under Bank in about 1880. The three figures on the outside of the building strike bells every 15 minutes. Security-conscious Winter had the contents of his shop windows displayed on a stage system that could be lowered into the cellar by means of a hydraulic lift; it was operated by natural spring water.

◆

CHEADLE
The Church c1960

The church is mainly 16th-century. The chapel was completed around 1530, the nave c1541, and the tower over the period 1520-1540. The chancel was rebuilt by Lady Catherine Buckley in the 1550s and the porch is dated 1634. Six of the bells were supplied by Rudhall of Gloucester in 1749, and two further bells were added in 1882.

STOCKPORT, LITTLE UNDER BANK 1968 S267014

CHEADLE, THE CHURCH c1960 C536047

CHEADLE, THE WHITE HART HOTEL c1965 C536034

The church was renovated in the mid 1860s. It was also famed for its absentee rectors, including Edward Trafford Leigh, who took himself off to Italy for his health in the 1830s. Another absentee rector put in a total of just six months' work during an incumbency lasting eight years; he claimed he was suffering from work-related stress.

CHEADLE HULME, STATION ROAD c1955 C285022

Cheadle Hulme is part of a township which includes Cheadle Bulkeley and Cheadle Moseley, which became a parish in its own right in August 1868. The view is looking towards the former London & North Western Railway station on the line to Stockport and Manchester. Note also the roadside petrol pumps, now collectors' items in their own right.

BRAMHALL, BRAMHALL LANE c1960 B360030

Hazel Grove-cum-Bramhall became a civil parish in 1900; it was made up from the older parishes of Bosden, Norbury, Offerton, Torkington, and Bramhall. About 50 years before this picture was taken, there were at least two farms off Bramhall Lane, as well as Miss Hooley's private school, Bramhall Grammar School, the consulting rooms of two physicians and surgeons, a post office, fishmonger and fruiterers, a confectioner, a grocers, a boot maker and cycle dealer, and a branch of the Lancashire & Yorkshire bank.

GATLEY, GATLEY ROAD c1955 G126024

Once a small village just a few miles west-south-west of Stockport, Gatley was chosen in the 1840s as the site for the Manchester Royal Lunatic Hospital. The hospital was enlarged in 1885 and again in 1897.

GATLEY, THE PARISH CHURCH AND THE PRINCE OF WALES HOTEL
c1955 G126004

GATLEY
*The Parish Church
and the Prince of Wales Hotel c1955*
Built of red brick, the church of
St James the Apostle was erected in 1881
with seating for 250 parishioners. When
built, it consisted of a chancel, nave,
transepts, and an unusual
saddle-back tower.

◆

ALTRINCHAM
The Town Hall 1903
Designed in the Jacobean style by the
Manchester firm of Hindle & Davenport,
the Town Hall was built in 1901 to
replace an earlier one situated in the
Market Place. Built in red brick with red
sandstone dressings, the Town Hall was
noted for its panelled ceiling and
stained glass windows in the
council chamber.

ALTRINCHAM, THE TOWN HALL 1903 49667

ALTRINCHAM, STAMFORD NEW ROAD 1903 49664
Altrincham is situated only 8 miles south-south-west of Manchester, and its popularity as a residential area for business people grew with the opening of the Manchester South Junction & Altrincham Railway. By the beginning of the 20th century, the town's population of 16,800 was served by no fewer than four railway stations; Altrincham & Bowdon, Hale, Broadheath, and West Timperley.

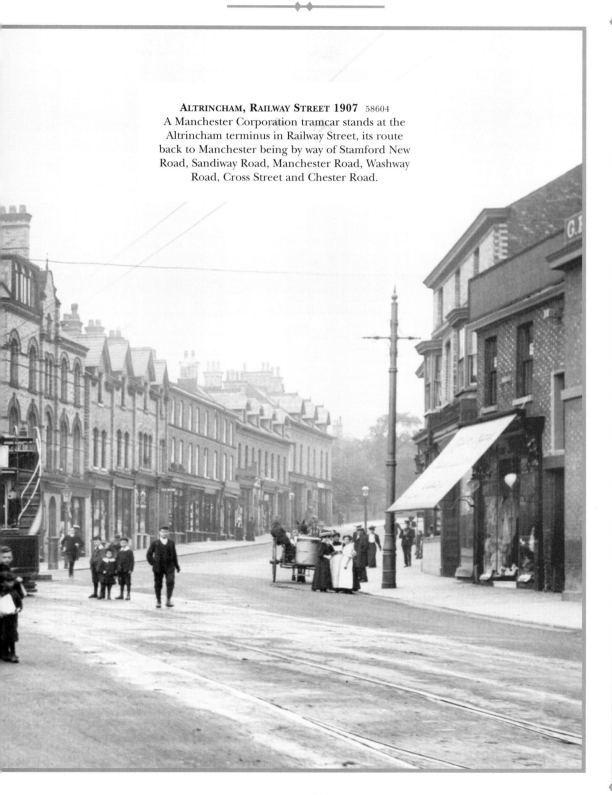

ALTRINCHAM, RAILWAY STREET 1907 58604
A Manchester Corporation tramcar stands at the Altrincham terminus in Railway Street, its route back to Manchester being by way of Stamford New Road, Sandiway Road, Manchester Road, Washway Road, Cross Street and Chester Road.

ALTRINCHAM, GEORGE STREET 1900 45448
This was one of the principal shopping streets of the town, though the Methodist New Connection chapel and the Salvation Army Hall were also along here. Some of the businesses seen here include Mason's (hosiers and hatters) at number 85, George Roberts & Sons (butchers) at number 89, and china dealer John Ingham at number 93.

ALTRINCHAM, THE OLD BANK 1897 39064

Carriages await the call to duty in the old Market Place; it was here that B Goodall & Co, bus and carriage proprietors, had their office, though we do not know if the vehicles seen here all belonged to them. Though most people would have taken the train to Manchester, a Goodall carriage hired to take 3-4 persons would have cost about 9s for the trip. If required to wait and then bring the clients back to Altrincham, it would be charged out by the hour.

TIMPERLEY, THE CHURCH 1898 42116

The scattered village of Timperley became a parish in its own right in 1852. Christ Church was consecrated in 1849 and enlarged in 1864. It is built of Runcorn freestone and is noted for its mixture of styles. This photograph pre-dates the building of the vestry, which was added in 1900.

WARBURTON, THE IRON BRIDGE 1897 39051
At this time Warburton was a small village on the south bank of the Mersey, five miles west of Altrincham and twelve miles from Manchester. The iron bridge was erected 1864-65 to connect the village with Lancashire.

WARBURTON, THE OLD CHURCH 1897 39052
Even at this time the old church dedicated to St Werburgh saw only weekday services and funerals. An ancient timber-frame building comprising a chancel, nave of four bays, aisles, south transept, and an east tower with just one bell, it had been repaired with stone during the 17th century. In 1885 R E Egerton-Warburton paid for a new church to be built.

HALE, VICTORIA ROAD 1907 58620

Try standing in the middle of the main street nowadays! Here at number 28 we have Joseph Kennerley's drapery and hosiery shop, which also doubled as the post office. The business must have recently changed hands, because in the 1906 directory it was the premises of Charles Riley, and Kennerley's shop was at 112 and 114 Ashley Road. Next door at number 26 is a sub-branch of the Union Bank of Manchester, whilst further along is Ward's greengrocers and Rogers' chemist and druggist store.

HALE, ASHLEY ROAD c1955 H226002
A lady checks her list as she makes her rounds of the shops. At this time shoppers could expect to pay about 1s 4d for 2lb of sugar, 2s 11d for a lb of streaky bacon, 3s 10d for a dozen eggs, and 4d for a 14oz loaf.

HALE, THE OLD BLEEDING WOLF 1913 66057
A soldier stands smartly to attention while our cameraman takes his picture. The soldier is in his best uniform and is probably on his way to the drill hall in Ashley Road, depot for A and B companies of the 1st Volunteer Battalion, Cheshire Regiment. Who knows - perhaps our photographer treated him to a swift pint in the Old Bleeding Wolf.

BOWDON, THE PARISH CHURCH 1889 21917
Dedicated to the Blessed Virgin Mary, the 14th-century parish church was rebuilt between 1858 and 1860 at a cost of £15,000; some 14th-century roof timbers were salvaged and reused. The earliest monument is claimed by some to be a 10th-century representation of Christ.

BOWDON, THE PARISH CHURCH 1913 66070A
This view shows the four-stage west tower. Because of the height of the clerestory, the east-facing clock face had to be sited higher up the tower than those on the other sides. The architect responsible for the rebuilding St Mary's was W H Brakespeare, who, in the 1870s, also designed the since-demolished St Paul's Methodist Church, Enville Road.

BOWDON, THE POLYGON, STAMFORD ROAD 1907 58602
The row of shops opposite was known as The Polygon,
though R H Toothill's chemist shop is on Church View.
Retailers listed as having businesses here in 1907 are
Brook & Son, grocers and agents for W & A Gilbey Ltd,
wine and spirit merchants; Goulden Bros, fruiterers
and florists; Alfred Pickering, confectioner;
and John Sydney Wykes, bootmaker.

BOWDON, THE CHURCH 1913 66079
With the opening of the railway in 1849, Bowdon soon became a popular residential area for wealthy Mancunians; the area around the church was particularly favoured during the 1850s.

BOWDON, SOUTH DOWN ROAD 1897 39071

This cottage was well over three hundred years old when the Frith cameraman took this picture. Kelly's Directory for 1906 lists a South Downs Cottage, which at the time was the residence of a Mr Frederick Bernard Yahr. At this time residences along South Down Road had names, not numbers; Samuel George Isherwood was living at Villaverde; Alfred Talbolton, JP at Athelney; Mrs Speigelburg at The Coppice; and John B Laycock at Rylstone.

BOWDON, PARK ROAD 1897 39062

From one of these fine thatched cottages John Hassell plied his trade as a porter. John was still there in 1906; his is the only address on the road that appears in the commercial section of that year's Kelly's Directory. John's neighbour at the vicarage was Canon Arthur Gore DD, who was vicar surrogate and canon residentiary of Chester, and examining chaplain to the Bishop of Chester.

BOWDON, DUNHAM MILL 1892 30392
Dunham Mill dates back to the medieval period; it was one of only a handful of mills in this part of Cheshire.

SALE, NORTHENDEN ROAD c1965 S344025

Northenden Road was one of Sale's main streets for shops, along with Chapel Road, School Road and Washway Road. About sixty years before this picture was taken Northenden Road was home to plumbers, gardeners, and builders. Among the shops along here at that time were Alexander Grey (ironmonger), Victor Flint (fishmonger), Mrs Letitia Archibald (draper and stationer), Mrs Annie Augenault (confectioner), John Clark (hairdresser), and Alfred Frape (draper).

SALE, THE TOWN HALL c1955 S344002

In 1892 the town's sewage works was opened. It was a state-of-the-art facility, so whatever the residents of Sale flushed down their loos was chemically purified before it was pumped into the Mersey (up to 750,000 gallons a day); the sludge was sold for fertilizer.

FLIXTON, FLIXTON ROAD c1960 F162009
An old village on the Cheshire side of the Manchester Ship Canal, Flixton was developed as a residential suburb of Manchester. Two interesting residents in the local churchyard are John and Hannah Booth. John was the village fiddler, and he and his wife died within hours of one another on the same day in 1778.

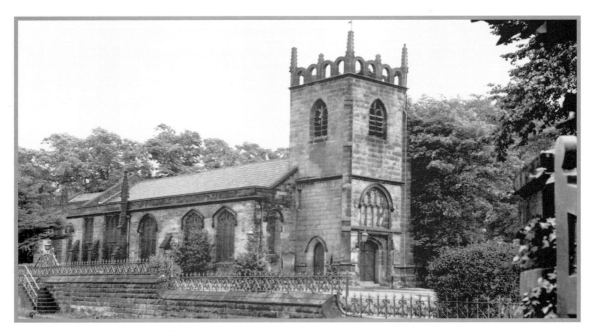

DIDSBURY, PARISH CHURCH c1955 D106001
St James's, Skinner Lane was remodelled no less than three times during the 19th century, in 1855, 1871 (chancel) and 1895 (south aisle). The west tower with its openwork loops dates from 1620, and is an earlier rebuilding. Inside is a monument to Sir Nicholas Mosley (1612), his two wives and children.

Index

Frith Book Co Titles

www.francisfrith.co.uk

The Frith Book Company publishes over 100 new titles each year. A selection of those currently available are listed below. For latest catalogue please contact Frith Book Co.
Town Books 96 pages, approximately 100 photos. **County and Themed Books** 128 pages, approximately 150 photos (unless specified). All titles hardback with laminated case and jacket, except those indicated pb (paperback)

Amersham, Chesham & Rickmansworth (pb)	1-85937-340-2	£9.99	Devon (pb)	1-85937-297-x	£9.99
Andover (pb)	1-85937-292-9	£9.99	Devon Churches (pb)	1-85937-250-3	£9.99
Aylesbury (pb)	1-85937-227-9	£9.99	Dorchester (pb)	1-85937-307-0	£9.99
Barnstaple (pb)	1-85937-300-3	£9.99	Dorset (pb)	1-85937-269-4	£9.99
Basildon Living Memories (pb)	1-85937-515-4	£9.99	Dorset Coast (pb)	1-85937-299-6	£9.99
Bath (pb)	1-85937-419-0	£9.99	Dorset Living Memories (pb)	1-85937-584-7	£9.99
Bedford (pb)	1-85937-205-8	£9.99	Down the Severn (pb)	1-85937-560-x	£9.99
Bedfordshire Living Memories	1-85937-513-8	£14.99	Down The Thames (pb)	1-85937-278-3	£9.99
Belfast (pb)	1-85937-303-8	£9.99	Down the Trent	1-85937-311-9	£14.99
Berkshire (pb)	1-85937-191-4	£9.99	East Anglia (pb)	1-85937-265-1	£9.99
Berkshire Churches	1-85937-170-1	£17.99	East Grinstead (pb)	1-85937-138-8	£9.99
Berkshire Living Memories	1-85937-332-1	£14.99	East London	1-85937-080-2	£14.99
Black Country	1-85937-497-2	£12.99	East Sussex (pb)	1-85937-606-1	£9.99
Blackpool (pb)	1-85937-393-3	£9.99	Eastbourne (pb)	1-85937-399-2	£9.99
Bognor Regis (pb)	1-85937-431-x	£9.99	Edinburgh (pb)	1-85937-193-0	£8.99
Bournemouth (pb)	1-85937-545-6	£9.99	England In The 1880s	1-85937-331-3	£17.99
Bradford (pb)	1-85937-204-x	£9.99	Essex - Second Selection	1-85937-456-5	£14.99
Bridgend (pb)	1-85937-386-0	£7.99	Essex (pb)	1-85937-270-8	£9.99
Bridgwater (pb)	1-85937-305-4	£9.99	Essex Coast	1-85937-342-9	£14.99
Bridport (pb)	1-85937-327-5	£9.99	Essex Living Memories	1-85937-490-5	£14.99
Brighton (pb)	1-85937-192-2	£8.99	Exeter	1-85937-539-1	£9.99
Bristol (pb)	1-85937-264-3	£9.99	Exmoor (pb)	1-85937-608-8	£9.99
British Life A Century Ago (pb)	1-85937-213-9	£9.99	Falmouth (pb)	1-85937-594-4	£9.99
Buckinghamshire (pb)	1-85937-200-7	£9.99	Folkestone (pb)	1-85937-124-8	£9.99
Camberley (pb)	1-85937-222-8	£9.99	Frome (pb)	1-85937-317-8	£9.99
Cambridge (pb)	1-85937-422-0	£9.99	Glamorgan	1-85937-488-3	£14.99
Cambridgeshire (pb)	1-85937-420-4	£9.99	Glasgow (pb)	1-85937-190-6	£9.99
Cambridgeshire Villages	1-85937-523-5	£14.99	Glastonbury (pb)	1-85937-338-0	£7.99
Canals And Waterways (pb)	1-85937-291-0	£9.99	Gloucester (pb)	1-85937-232-5	£9.99
Canterbury Cathedral (pb)	1-85937-179-5	£9.99	Gloucestershire (pb)	1-85937-561-8	£9.99
Cardiff (pb)	1-85937-093-4	£9.99	Great Yarmouth (pb)	1-85937-426-3	£9.99
Carmarthenshire (pb)	1-85937-604-5	£9.99	Greater Manchester (pb)	1-85937-266-x	£9.99
Chelmsford (pb)	1-85937-310-0	£9.99	Guildford (pb)	1-85937-410-7	£9.99
Cheltenham (pb)	1-85937-095-0	£9.99	Hampshire (pb)	1-85937-279-1	£9.99
Cheshire (pb)	1-85937-271-6	£9.99	Harrogate (pb)	1-85937-423-9	£9.99
Chester (pb)	1-85937-382 8	£9.99	Hastings and Bexhill (pb)	1-85937-131-0	£9.99
Chesterfield (pb)	1-85937-378-x	£9.99	Heart of Lancashire (pb)	1-85937-197-3	£9.99
Chichester (pb)	1-85937-228-7	£9.99	Helston (pb)	1-85937-214-7	£9.99
Churches of East Cornwall (pb)	1-85937-249-x	£9.99	Hereford (pb)	1-85937-175-2	£9.99
Churches of Hampshire (pb)	1-85937-207-4	£9.99	Herefordshire (pb)	1-85937-567-7	£9.99
Cinque Ports & Two Ancient Towns	1-85937-492-1	£14.99	Herefordshire Living Memories	1-85937-514-6	£14.99
Colchester (pb)	1-85937-188-4	£8.99	Hertfordshire (pb)	1-85937-247-3	£9.99
Cornwall (pb)	1-85937-229-5	£9.99	Horsham (pb)	1-85937-432-8	£9.99
Cornwall Living Memories	1-85937-248-1	£14.99	Humberside (pb)	1-85937-605-3	£9.99
Cotswolds (pb)	1-85937-230-9	£9.99	Hythe, Romney Marsh, Ashford (pb)	1-85937-256-2	£9.99
Cotswolds Living Memories	1-85937-255-4	£14.99	Ipswich (pb)	1-85937-424-7	£9.99
County Durham (pb)	1-85937-398-4	£9.99	Isle of Man (pb)	1-85937-268-6	£9.99
Croydon Living Memories (pb)	1-85937-162-0	£9.99	Isle of Wight (pb)	1-85937-429-8	£9.99
Cumbria (pb)	1-85937-621-5	£9.99	Isle of Wight Living Memories	1-85937-304-6	£14.99
Derby (pb)	1-85937-367-4	£9.99	Kent (pb)	1-85937-189-2	£9.99
Derbyshire (pb)	1-85937-196-5	£9.99	Kent Living Memories(pb)	1-85937-401-8	£9.99
Derbyshire Living Memories	1-85937-330-5	£14.99	Kings Lynn (pb)	1-85937-334-8	£9.99

Available from your local bookshop or from the publisher

Frith Book Co Titles (continued)

Title	ISBN	Price	Title	ISBN	Price
Lake District (pb)	1-85937-275-9	£9.99	Sherborne (pb)	1-85937-301-1	£9.99
Lancashire Living Memories	1-85937-335-6	£14.99	Shrewsbury (pb)	1-85937-325-9	£9.99
Lancaster, Morecambe, Heysham (pb)	1-85937-233-3	£9.99	Shropshire (pb)	1-85937-326-7	£9.99
Leeds (pb)	1-85937-202-3	£9.99	Shropshire Living Memories	1-85937-643-6	£14.99
Leicester (pb)	1-85937-381-x	£9.99	Somerset	1-85937-153-1	£14.99
Leicestershire & Rutland Living Memories	1-85937-500-6	£12.99	South Devon Coast	1-85937-107-8	£14.99
Leicestershire (pb)	1-85937-185-x	£9.99	South Devon Living Memories (pb)	1-85937-609-6	£9.99
Lighthouses	1-85937-257-0	£9.99	South East London (pb)	1-85937-263-5	£9.99
Lincoln (pb)	1-85937-380-1	£9.99	South Somerset	1-85937-318-6	£14.99
Lincolnshire (pb)	1-85937-433-6	£9.99	South Wales	1-85937-519-7	£14.99
Liverpool and Merseyside (pb)	1-85937-234-1	£9.99	Southampton (pb)	1-85937-427-1	£9.99
London (pb)	1-85937-183-3	£9.99	Southend (pb)	1-85937-313-5	£9.99
London Living Memories	1-85937-454-9	£14.99	Southport (pb)	1-85937-425-5	£9.99
Ludlow (pb)	1-85937-176-0	£9.99	St Albans (pb)	1-85937-341-0	£9.99
Luton (pb)	1-85937-235-x	£9.99	St Ives (pb)	1-85937-415-8	£9.99
Maidenhead (pb)	1-85937-339-9	£9.99	Stafford Living Memories (pb)	1-85937-503-0	£9.99
Maidstone (pb)	1-85937-391-7	£9.99	Staffordshire (pb)	1-85937-308-9	£9.99
Manchester (pb)	1-85937-198-1	£9.99	Stourbridge (pb)	1-85937-530-8	£9.99
Marlborough (pb)	1-85937-336-4	£9.99	Stratford upon Avon (pb)	1-85937-388-7	£9.99
Middlesex	1-85937-158-2	£14.99	Suffolk (pb)	1-85937-221-x	£9.99
Monmouthshire	1-85937-532-4	£14.99	Suffolk Coast (pb)	1-85937-610-x	£9.99
New Forest (pb)	1-85937-390-9	£9.99	Surrey (pb)	1-85937-240-6	£9.99
Newark (pb)	1-85937-366-6	£9.99	Surrey Living Memories	1-85937-328-3	£14.99
Newport, Wales (pb)	1-85937-258-9	£9.99	Sussex (pb)	1-85937-184-1	£9.99
Newquay (pb)	1-85937-421-2	£9.99	Sutton (pb)	1-85937-337-2	£9.99
Norfolk (pb)	1-85937-195-7	£9.99	Swansea (pb)	1-85937-167-1	£9.99
Norfolk Broads	1-85937-486-7	£14.99	Taunton (pb)	1-85937-314-3	£9.99
Norfolk Living Memories (pb)	1-85937-402-6	£9.99	Tees Valley & Cleveland (pb)	1-85937-623-1	£9.99
North Buckinghamshire	1-85937-626-6	£14.99	Teignmouth (pb)	1-85937-370-4	£7.99
North Devon Living Memories	1-85937-261-9	£14.99	Thanet (pb)	1-85937-116-7	£9.99
North Hertfordshire	1-85937-547-2	£14.99	Tiverton (pb)	1-85937-178-7	£9.99
North London (pb)	1-85937-403-4	£9.99	Torbay (pb)	1-85937-597-9	£9.99
North Somerset	1-85937-302-x	£14.99	Truro (pb)	1-85937-598-7	£9.99
North Wales (pb)	1-85937-298-8	£9.99	Victorian & Edwardian Dorset	1-85937-254-6	£14.99
North Yorkshire (pb)	1-85937-236-8	£9.99	Victorian & Edwardian Kent (pb)	1-85937-624-X	£9.99
Northamptonshire Living Memories	1-85937-529-4	£14.99	Victorian & Edwardian Maritime Album (pb)	1-85937-622-3	£9.99
Northamptonshire	1-85937-150-7	£14.99	Victorian and Edwardian Sussex (pb)	1-85937-625-8	£9.99
Northumberland Tyne & Wear (pb)	1-85937-281-3	£9.99	Villages of Devon (pb)	1-85937-293-7	£9.99
Northumberland	1-85937-522-7	£14.99	Villages of Kent (pb)	1-85937-294-5	£9.99
Norwich (pb)	1-85937-194-9	£8.99	Villages of Sussex (pb)	1-85937-295-3	£9.99
Nottingham (pb)	1-85937-324-0	£9.99	Warrington (pb)	1-85937-507-3	£9.99
Nottinghamshire (pb)	1-85937-187-6	£9.99	Warwick (pb)	1-85937-518-9	£9.99
Oxford (pb)	1-85937-411-5	£9.99	Warwickshire (pb)	1-85937-203-1	£9.99
Oxfordshire (pb)	1-85937-430-1	£9.99	Welsh Castles (pb)	1-85937-322-4	£9.99
Oxfordshire Living Memories	1-85937-525-1	£14.99	West Midlands (pb)	1-85937-289-9	£9.99
Paignton (pb)	1-85937-374-7	£7.99	West Sussex (pb)	1-85937-607-x	£9.99
Peak District (pb)	1-85937-280-5	£9.99	West Yorkshire (pb)	1-85937-201-5	£9.99
Pembrokeshire	1-85937-262-7	£14.99	Weston Super Mare (pb)	1-85937-306-2	£9.99
Penzance (pb)	1-85937-595-2	£9.99	Weymouth (pb)	1-85937-209-0	£9.99
Peterborough (pb)	1-85937-219-8	£9.99	Wiltshire (pb)	1-85937-277-5	£9.99
Picturesque Harbours	1-85937-208-2	£14.99	Wiltshire Churches (pb)	1-85937-171-x	£9.99
Piers	1-85937-237-6	£17.99	Wiltshire Living Memories (pb)	1-85937-396-8	£9.99
Plymouth (pb)	1-85937-389-5	£9.99	Winchester (pb)	1-85937-428-x	£9.99
Poole & Sandbanks (pb)	1-85937-251-1	£9.99	Windsor (pb)	1-85937-333-x	£9.99
Preston (pb)	1-85937-212-0	£9.99	Wokingham & Bracknell (pb)	1-85937-329-1	£9.99
Reading (pb)	1-85937-238-4	£9.99	Woodbridge (pb)	1-85937-498-0	£9.99
Redhill to Reigate (pb)	1-85937-596-0	£9.99	Worcester (pb)	1-85937-165-5	£9.99
Ringwood (pb)	1-85937-384-4	£7.99	Worcestershire Living Memories	1-85937-489-1	£14.99
Romford (pb)	1-85937-319-4	£9.99	Worcestershire	1-85937-152-3	£14.99
Royal Tunbridge Wells (pb)	1-85937-504-9	£9.99	York (pb)	1-85937-199-x	£9.99
Salisbury (pb)	1-85937-239-2	£9.99	Yorkshire (pb)	1-85937-186-8	£9.99
Scarborough (pb)	1-85937-379-8	£9.99	Yorkshire Coastal Memories	1-85937-506-5	£14.99
Sevenoaks and Tonbridge (pb)	1-85937-392-5	£9.99	Yorkshire Dales	1-85937-502-2	£14.99
Sheffield & South Yorks (pb)	1-85937-267-8	£9.99	Yorkshire Living Memories (pb)	1-85937-397-6	£9.99

See Frith books on the internet at www.francisfrith.co.uk

FRITH PRODUCTS & SERVICES

Francis Frith would doubtless be pleased to know that the pioneering publishing venture he started in 1860 still continues today. Over a hundred and forty years later, The Francis Frith Collection continues in the same innovative tradition and is now one of the foremost publishers of vintage photographs in the world. Some of the current activities include:

Interior Decoration

Today Frith's photographs can be seen framed and as giant wall murals in thousands of pubs, restaurants, hotels, banks, retail stores and other public buildings throughout the country. In every case they enhance the unique local atmosphere of the places they depict and provide reminders of gentler days in an increasingly busy and frenetic world.

Product Promotions

Frith products are used by many major companies to promote the sales of their own products or to reinforce their own history and heritage. Frith promotions have been used by Hovis bread, Courage beers, Scots Porage Oats, Colman's mustard, Cadbury's foods, Mellow Birds coffee, Dunhill pipe tobacco, Guinness, and Bulmer's Cider.

Genealogy and Family History

As the interest in family history and roots grows world-wide, more and more people are turning to Frith's photographs of Great Britain for images of the towns, villages and streets where their ancestors lived; and, of course, photographs of the churches and chapels where their ancestors were christened, married and buried are an essential part of every genealogy tree and family album.

Frith Products

All Frith photographs are available Framed or just as Mounted Prints and Posters (size 23 x 16 inches). These may be ordered from the address below. From time to time other products - Address Books, Calendars, Table Mats, etc - are available.

The Internet

Already fifty thousand Frith photographs can be viewed and purchased on the internet through the Frith websites and a myriad of partner sites.

For more detailed information on Frith companies and products, look at these sites:

www.francisfrith.co.uk
www.francisfrith.com
(for North American visitors)

See the complete list of Frith Books at:

www.francisfrith.co.uk

This web site is regularly updated with the latest list of publications from the Frith Book Company. If you wish to buy books relating to another part of the country that your local bookshop does not stock, you may purchase on-line.

For further information, trade, or author enquiries please contact us at the address below:
The Francis Frith Collection, Frith's Barn, Teffont, Salisbury, Wiltshire, England SP3 5QP.
Tel: +44 (0)1722 716 376 Fax: +44 (0)1722 716 881   Email: sales@francisfrith.co.uk

See Frith books on the internet at www.francisfrith.co.uk

HOW TO ORDER YOUR FREE MOUNTED PRINT
and other Frith prints at half price

Mounted Print
Overall size 14 x 11 inches

Fill in and cut out this voucher and return it with your remittance for £2.25 (to cover postage and handling to UK addresses). For overseas addresses please include £4.00 post and handling.
Choose any photograph included in this book. Your SEPIA print will be A4 in size. It will be mounted in a cream mount with a burgundy rule line (overall size 14 x 11 inches).

Order additional Mounted Prints at HALF PRICE (only £7.49 each*)
If you would like to order more Frith prints from this book, possibly as gifts for friends and family, you can buy them at half price (with no additional postage and handling costs).

Have your Mounted Prints framed
For an extra £14.95 per print* you can have your mounted print(s) framed in an elegant polished wood and gilt moulding, overall size 16 x 13 inches (no additional postage and handling required).

---

* IMPORTANT!

These special prices are only available if you order at the same time as you order your free mounted print. You must use the ORIGINAL VOUCHER on this page (no copies permitted). We can only despatch to one address.

Voucher *for FREE and Reduced Price Frith Prints*

Please do not photocopy this voucher. Only the original is valid, so please fill it in, cut it out and return it to us with your order.

Picture ref no	Page number	Qty	Mounted @ £7.49	Framed + £14.95	Total Cost
		1	Free of charge*	£	£
			£7.49	£	£
			£7.49	£	£
			£7.49	£	£
			£7.49	£	£
			£7.49	£	£
Please allow 28 days for delivery			* Post & handling (UK)		£2.25
			Total Order Cost		£

Title of this book . . . .

I enclose a cheque/postal order for £ . . . .
made payable to 'The Francis Frith Collection'

OR please debit my Mastercard / Visa / Switch / Amex card
(credit cards please on all overseas orders), details below

Card Number

Issue No (Switch only)   Valid from (Amex/Switch)

Expires   Signature

Name Mr/Mrs/Ms . . . .

Address . . . .
. . . .
. . . .
. . . . Postcode . . . .

Daytime Tel No . . . .

Email . . . .

Valid to 31/12/05

Send completed Voucher form to:
The Francis Frith Collection, Frith's Barn, Teffont, Salisbury, Wiltshire SP3 5QP

Would you like to find out more about Francis Frith?

We have recently recruited some entertaining speakers who are happy to visit local groups, clubs and societies to give an illustrated talk documenting Frith's travels and photographs. If you are a member of such a group and are interested in hosting a presentation, we would love to hear from you.

Our speakers bring with them a small selection of our local town and county books, together with sample prints. They are happy to take orders. A small proportion of the order value is donated to the group who have hosted the presentation. The talks are therefore an excellent way of fundraising for small groups and societies.

Can you help us with information about any of the Frith photographs in this book?

We are gradually compiling an historical record for each of the photographs in the Frith archive. It is always fascinating to find out the names of the people shown in the pictures, as well as insights into the shops, buildings and other features depicted.

If you recognize anyone in the photographs in this book, or if you have information not already included in the author's caption, do let us know. We would love to hear from you, and will try to publish it in future books or articles.

Our production team

Frith books are produced by a small dedicated team at offices in the converted Grade II listed 18th-century barn at Teffont near Salisbury, illustrated above. Most have worked with the Frith Collection for many years. All have in common one quality: they have a passion for the Frith Collection. The team is constantly expanding, but currently includes:

Jason Buck, John Buck, Douglas Burns, Ruth Butler, Heather Crisp, Isobel Hall, Hazel Heaton, Peter Horne, James Kinnear, Tina Leary, Sue Molloy, Hannah Marsh, Kate Rotondetto, Dean Scource, Eliza Sackett, Terence Sackett, Sandra Sanger, Lewis Taylor, and Shelley Tolcher.